SOVIET UNION: THE CHALLENGE OF CHANGE

SOVIET UNION: THE CHALLENGE OF CHANGE

COUNTRIES IN CRISIS

Edited by
MARTIN WRIGHT

**Contributors: Sir Bryan Cartledge, Stephen Dalziel,
David Dyker, Ian Gorvin, Angus Macqueen,
Tim Whewell, Helen Womack and Martin Wright**

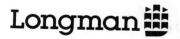

SOVIET UNION: THE CHALLENGE OF CHANGE

Published by Longman Group UK Limited,
Westgate House, The High, Harlow, Essex CM20 1YR, UK.
Telephone (0279) 442601
Telex 81491 Padlog
Facsimile (0279) 444501

Published in the United States and Canada by St James Press,
233 East Ontario St, Chicago 60611, Illinois, U.S.A.

ISBN 0-582-05155-X   (Longman, hard cover)
     0-582-05158-4   (Longman, paper cover)

     1-55862-029-X   (St James)

First published in 1989

British Library Cataloguing in Publication Data
Wright, Martin, 1958–
    Soviet Union: the challenge of change.
    —(Countries in crisis)
    1. Soviet Union. Politics
    I. Title   II. Series
    320.947

    ISBN 0-582-05155-X
    ISBN 0-582-05158-4 pbk

Phototypeset by Quorn Selective Repro Ltd, Loughborough, Leics.
Printed and bound in Great Britain by
Biddles Ltd, Guildford and King's Lynn

CONTENTS

REPORTAGE

ABOUT THE AUTHORS

Sir Bryan Cartledge is a former diplomat who served as British Ambassador to Moscow until late 1988. He is currently Principal of Linacre College, Oxford.

Stephen Dalziel was Senior Lecturer at the Soviet Studies Research Centre at the Royal Military Academy at Sandhurst until 1988, when he joined the BBC World Service as a commentator on Soviet Affairs.

David Dyker is Senior Lecturer in Economics at the School of European Studies, University of Sussex. He has written widely on Soviet affairs, and edited *The Soviet Union Under Gorbachev: Prospects for Reform* (Croom Helm, 1987).

Ian Gorvin writes on Soviet and East European affairs for *Keesing's Record of World Events*. He has lived and worked in Moscow.

Angus Macqueen is a freelance television researcher specializing in the Soviet Union and Eastern Europe. He has previously worked as a lecturer in Novosibirsk University.

Tim Whewell is a scriptwriter for the Russian Service of the BBC. He has travelled widely within the Soviet Union.

Helen Womack worked in Moscow for the Reuters news agency in 1985–88, after which she joined the foreign staff of *The Independent*. She is married to a Soviet citizen.

Martin Wright is editor of the *Countries in Crisis* series. Formerly on the staff of *Keesing's Record of World Events*, he now works as a publishing consultant and freelance journalist.

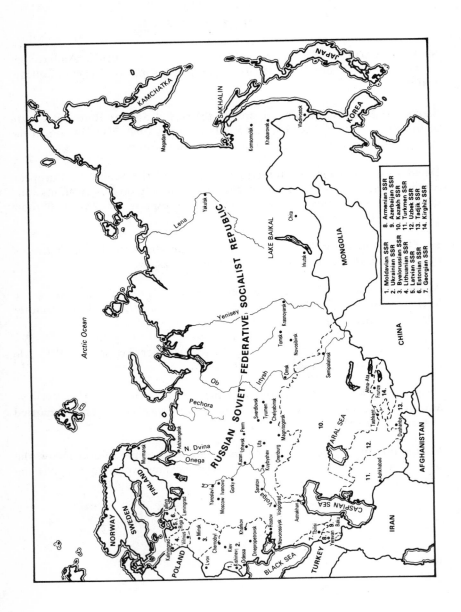

PREFACE

Under the leadership of Mikhail Gorbachev, the Soviet Union is undergoing some of the most dramatic changes since the revolution. To some extent at least, what Gorbachev is attempting amounts to nothing short of a second revolution, involving a fundamental restructuring of the Soviet political system. If he succeeds, the country could emerge with a robust economy and a workable, popular democracy—something unthinkable only a decade ago. On the other hand, the consequences of failure might, at best, be a return to the corrupt stagnation of the Brezhnev era—at worst, a slide into political chaos and economic collapse.

This book provides a clear, readable account of the Gorbachev revolution. In Part I, a brief historical summary of the growth of Russia and the first 60 years of the Soviet regime leads into a detailed survey of the Gorbachev years. Separate chapters chart the fortunes of *glasnost* and *perestroika*, of the political battles with the conservative "old guard"; they report on the rising tide of nationalism in the Baltic Republics and elsewhere, of the implications of reform in the Soviet Union for its Eastern European allies, and of the changing face of Soviet foreign policy.

In Part II, leading commentators on Soviet affairs examine the critical decisions facing Mikhail Gorbachev and the Soviet leadership, assess the extent of popular support for their reforms, and look at the likely consequences for the future. Throughout the book, the Reportage features lift the mask of politics to give a glimpse of the impact of events on everyday life in the Soviet Union.

Acknowledgements The front cover photograph, by J. Arthur, was provided by Reflex Picture Agency. Permission for the use of this photograph and others appearing in the text by Dod Miller and Liba Taylor for Select Photo Agency, and by Y. Goligorsky and Angus Macqueen, is gratefully acknowledged. Copyright remains with the Agencies/photographers.

SOVIET UNION: INFRASTRUCTURE

The Union of Soviet Socialist Republics is the largest country in the world. With an area of over 22 million sq km, it occupies one sixth of the earth's land surface. From the western frontier to the Bering Strait in the east is a distance of nearly 10,000 km, while from north to south it stretches nearly 5,000 km at the widest point. In the west the country is bordered by Norway, Finland, Poland, Czechoslovakia, Hungary, and Romania; to the south and east lie Turkey, Iran, Afghanistan, China, Mongolia and North Korea. Physically, the Soviet Union is characterized as much by monotonous uniformity of landscape over wide areas as by great contrasts between one region and another. The climate over most of the country is continental, with winter temperatures falling as low as −70 °C in parts of Siberia, and summer temperatures reaching as high as 50 °C in Central Asia, part of which is desert.

The population of the Soviet Union reached 280 million in mid-1986. Its distribution is extremely uneven, with some 70 per cent of the population being found in the western, European part of the country. The country has a highly complex ethnic and linguistic composition, with over 100 ethnic groups being recorded in the 1979 census. By far the most numerous are Russians, who alone make up just over 50 per cent of the population, followed by Ukrainians, who account for around 17 per cent; Turkic-speaking peoples (including Uzbeks, Turkmen, Kirgiz, Kazakhs, Azerbaijanis and Tatars) make up around 10 per cent. Russian is the official language, but altogether 112 recognized languages are spoken. Orthodox Christianity is the most widely practised religion, although there are also Moslem, Jewish, Buddhist and Shamanist communities, together with other Christian churches.

The Soviet Union is endowed with abundant fuel supplies and most industrial raw materials, although problems exist with their exploitation in remote areas. It is second only to the United States in terms of economic size and strength, and is the world's leading producer of petroleum, coal, iron ore, mineral fertilizers, cement and steel. However, it lags behind the Western industrial powers in terms of production processes, technical innovation and labour efficiency, while an emphasis on heavy industry has resulted in neglect of consumer goods production and consequent shortages.

Much of the Soviet Union's territory is unfavourable for agricultural development, principally because of the harsh climate. Only around 25 per cent of the total land area is used for agriculture, of which less than half is sown with crops, chiefly cereals. Over a third of the land is covered in forest; the Soviet Union is the world's leading producer of roundwood and sawnwood. Despite rapid urbanization in the past 60 years the rural population, at more than 40 per cent of the total, remains unusually large for a major industrial power.

Due to the sheer size of the country, the lion's share of freight and passenger transport is carried by rail: the extensive network inherited by the Soviet regime from Tsarist days has been increased threefold. Internal air services also play a major role in passenger transport, while inland waterways and coastal shipping routes are major freight carriers. Road transport is relatively underdeveloped, and with the exception of a number of modern, well-surfaced highways in the European part of the country, the road network remains rudimentary.

REPORTAGE

LENINGRAD STATION

Angus Macqueen

"No seats free to Mongolia, tonight," reads the sign in Leningrad's Moskva station. "The midnight express from Baku has just arrived on platform one." Trains are 800 minutes late. The expanse of Russia and the Soviet Union stretches out in the imagination—railway stations and departing trains make everything possible. Images of Alma Ata, Tblisi or Dushanbee are conjured up, sunny in the snowbound night. The eager adventurer starts playing "How to get there?" on the great rail map of the USSR in the station's main hall. Pick a destination, and lights will flash the route. The railway lines run dark and thick in the developed western parts of the country, unravelling into white space to the South and East, until one great spider's leg is cast across a continent to the Pacific Ocean, in an extended statement of possession.

Soviets proudly boast that they can see the world in one country—the Hanseatic charm of Tallinn (five hours from Leningrad), the vineyards and gorges of Georgia (two days), or a lake with one fifth of the world's fresh water, Baikal (eight days). It is all one state. For prying foreigners much remains closed "for reasons of security and state"—except of course to US military inspectors, or satellites. Unique cities, rivers and forests are off bounds to that most dangerous enemy, the tourist. This is changing: everyday the game of finding ways to Tomsk and Emba becomes more tantalisingly real.

Maybe now Yekaterinberg, or Nizhny Novgorod, an old bastion capital of Rus, towns whose historic names have been removed from maps to honour such giant revolutionary heroes as Sverdlovsk and Gorki, towns now making attempts to reclaim their earlier heritage. In pre-revolutionary days the map of the empire would have been about the same size as today's, and the railways surprisingly developed, but St Petersburg, not Moscow, would have been the centre—a centre on the margin, both hub and gateway. This glorious capital, built with as much deliberate planning as any steel works in the Soviet five-year plans, strove westwards with its canals, Italianate palaces and promenades, in a struggle between the Asian and the European which remains at the heart of the Russian identity. But, deprived of its power, and purged of its intelligensia during Stalin's terror, the beauty and the memories cannot offset the whiff of provincial status.

Consolation can be found in the station itself, which still draws in that dreamed-of hinterland. There are the permanently packed waiting rooms—grand halls with ornate ceilings and orange plastic chairs. Old peasant women, bundles of clothes and fat, cradle little children, dreaming of black-earth fields stretching to distant horizons; oriental faces stare out of dark spiky furs, motionless, as if engaged in meditation; bronzed Asians rest wiry frames upon their merchandise—nuts or melons mean straight profit, when sold in the pale frozen north. These are patient faces, blank and set. They may wait days for seats. With 10 hours or 10 days in the "hard" class of wooden bunks to come, time lost waiting, time won hurrying, matters less. Queues wind quietly across the ticket hall, or to the counter for sweet ersatz coffee and sticky buns. In the imagination, the musty still air momentarily holds a more resilient past intact.

Below there are the toilets. Descend into the bowels of the station, along dank sawdust-strewn corridors, clutching a five kopek coin that will gain you entrance (and maybe exit), and you may find another Leningrad. Male Leningrad at least. In the yellow half-light, two florid men in heavy coats, one sweating nervously, barter some watches under the benign eye of two policemen; a gaggle of drunks sway in corners at the entrance, bottles in hand, while others, no longer able to stand, sit in corners in the brown slush of melting snow on the floor. All are talking expansively, generating a drunken warmth amid wreaths of smoke—for this is the only place one is free to smoke. No threat (it seemed)—drugs have come to Leningrad, but not yet among souls who took to perfume when semi-prohibition meant the vodka ran out. Some are lost souls who in the Brezhnev years did not exist because "We have no homeless, no displaced, no problems". Now in the era of openness they will no doubt become statistics again.

Through the laughter and the acrid haze, the main toilet hall appears empty. Ranks of waist-high tile partitions line the right hand wall. You sense activity but you don't know where. From below a partition a fur hat with earflaps and drooping moustache emerges, rearranging his clothing. He looks purposeful, as he strides past, returning a newspaper (toilet paper) to his pocket. Perhaps he has a seat for those two weeks to Mongolia. Perhaps he's just arrived.

Young Moscow on parade (*Dod Miller/Select*)

Senior citizens out shopping (*Liba Taylor/Select*)

PART I: GORBACHEV'S SOVIET UNION: THE KEY ISSUES

BEFORE GORBACHEV

The first Russian state emerged towards the end of the ninth century, growing out of the Slav principalities which had developed along the river trade routes from the Baltic to the Black and Capsian Seas. These were gathered together by their Varangian (Norse) rulers into a loose federation known as Kievan Rus, with Kiev as its capital. Heavily influenced by Byzantium, Kievan Rus was converted to Orthodox Christianity in 988. It rapidly developed rich spiritual and cultural traditions surpassing those of many other European nations.

In the twelfth century Kievan Rus went into decline. Weakened by internal power struggles it fell prey to foreign assault. In 1237–40, the Russian principalities were invaded from the East by the Tatars, and for more than two centuries they came under Tatar overlordship as part of the vast Mongol-Tatar empire which stretched from eastern Europe to the Pacific. The period of the so-called "Tatar Yoke" witnessed increased migration away from the exposed southern steppe into the forests further north, where the Russians were relatively free from direct interference by the Tatars but were also isolated from the mainstream of European civilization.

The Russian principalities began to assert their independence in 1380 when they took up arms against the Tatars at the battle of Kulikovo Polye, and by the middle of the next century they had effectively thrown off Tatar overlordship; the payment of Russian tribute ceased around 1480. By this time Muscovy had emerged as paramount among the principalities, and during the reign of Grand Prince Ivan III (1462–1505) the absorption by Muscovy of the other independent principalities and of the republican city-states of Novgorod, Pskov and Vyatka began the process of territorial expansion which created the modern Russian state. By the mid-sixteenth century, Russia was expanding eastwards, across the Volga River towards the Ural mountains and Siberia.

Ivan III's grandson, Ivan IV ("The Terrible", who reigned from 1533–1584, and was the first to be proclaimed "Tsar of all the Russias") actively pursued expansion, capturing the Tatar Khanate of Kazan in 1552, and that of Astrakhan four years later.

Major westward expansion and the absorption of Western ideas began under the first Tsars of the Romanov dynasty, established on the throne of Muscovy in 1613. The greatest contribution to this westward orientation was made by Tsar Peter I ("The Great"), who reigned from 1696 to 1725. During this period Muscovy was formally renamed Russia and European customs and dress were adopted. It expanded westwards to the Baltic, and a new capital city, St Petersburg, was founded at the head of the Gulf of Finland to provide a "window on the west". Peter also originated the state administrative structure, including the system of ranked nobility, which survived until 1917. By the end of the reign of Catherine II ("The Great") in 1796, Russia was beginning to emerge as a major economic power through the annexation from Poland and Turkey of the rich agricultural lands of the Ukraine, Crimea and North Caucasus, which also gave access to the Black Sea.

After Napoleon's abortive invasion in 1812, his defeated forces were pursued out of Russia and across Europe to Paris by a Russian army headed by Alexander I (who had ascended the throne in 1801). This military campaign allowed Russia to claim a leading role on the European stage, but also brought about increased contact by younger members of the nobility with European forms of state and public institutions, giving rise to unfavourable comparisons with Russia's own system of government. Out of this developed the first stirrings of a revolutionary movement. In December 1825 a group of young noblemen (thereafter known as the "Decembrists") attempted a coup d'état during the interregnum between the death of Alexander and the installation as Tsar of his brother Nicholas. This failed, and the ensuing reign of Nicholas I became marked by an extremely reactionary and oppressive autocracy.

Nicholas's death in 1855 came one year before Russia's humiliating defeat in the Crimean War against Turkey, France and Great Britain. This débâcle led to a crisis of confidence in the existing order, prompting in turn major political and social reforms during the reign of Nicholas's son, Alexander II. The most striking of these, the emancipation of the serfs (peasants bonded to a private landlord), took place in 1861. Alexander's reign also saw an upsurge in political radicalism, with revolutionary movements such as the Populists becoming increasingly identified with anarchy and terrorism. On March 1, 1881, a populist group called "People's Will" assassinated the Tsar.

The main consequences of the assassination were a return to repressive autocracy under the new Tsar, Alexander III, and the discrediting of the

Populist movement. The latter gave impetus to emergent Russian Marxism: in 1883 the first Russian Marxist organization, the Emancipation of Labour Group, was founded by Georgy Plekhanov, and it was followed by the League of the Struggle for the Emancipation of the Working Class, formed by Vladimir Ilich Lenin in 1895. These and other Marxist groups merged in 1898 to form the Russian Social Democratic Labour Party at a secret congress in Minsk, but at the party's second congress held in Brussels and London in 1903 it split into two over Lenin's conception of the party as a highly centralized organization of professional revolutionaries. Lenin's supporters on this became known as Bolsheviks ("majoritarians") and opponents as Mensheviks ("minoritarians"). After failed attempts at reunification the Bolsheviks were established as a separate party in 1912.

Industrialization accelerated formidably during the 1890s, with growth rates in all branches of industry and production outstripping those of any other nation. Consequently, there was a rapid increase in the size of the urban working class, although this was heavily concentrated in the few main industrial areas and remained small compared to the rural population: at the end of the tsarist regime peasants still constituted more than three quarters of Russia's population.

In 1904 Russia entered into a disastrous war with Japan over spheres of influence in Manchuria and Korea. Towards the end of that year workers' unrest broke out in St Petersburg, and on Jan. 22, 1905, troops opened fire on a demonstration outside the Winter Palace, the residence of Tsar Nicholas II (who had ascended the throne in 1894). Some 150,000 people had gathered there to call for workers' rights and an end to the war. This sparked off a revolt throughout the country which lasted for most of the year and witnessed the appearance for the first time of revolutionary soviets (councils) of people's deputies. The 1905 revolution forced the Tsar at the end of October to proclaim a constitutional manifesto granting certain fundamental civil liberties and promising the creation of an elected parliament, the Duma, which met for the first time in May 1906.

WAR AND REVOLUTION

Russia entered the First World War against the Central Powers in August 1914, and was forced into retreat almost immediately. By the beginning of 1917 army morale was in a state of collapse, and when in March a wave of spontaneous demonstrations and strikes broke out in the capital (now renamed Petrograd), taking the authorities as well as the professional revolutionaries by surprise, troops mutinied in their tens of thousands. On March 15 Tsar Nicholas II abdicated in favour of his brother, Grand Duke Michael, but the latter refused the throne and a provisional government took power.

The provisional government forfeited popular support by attempting to continue the war, however, and its authority was challenged by the soviets of workers', peasants' and soldiers' deputies, which increasingly passed under Bolshevik control. On Nov. 7, 1917, the Bolsheviks seized power from the provisional government in a bloodless coup d'état, and established a Council of People's Commissars with Lenin as Chairman (Prime Minister). However, in elections to a Constituent Assembly held on Nov. 25 the Bolsheviks won only a quarter of the seats and an absolute majority went to the Socialist Revolutionaries. When a majority of deputies at the Assembly's opening session on Jan. 18, 1918, rejected Bolshevik demands that it should subordinate itself to the decisions of the Congress of Soviets, Bolsheviks and their supporters withdrew and the Bolshevik Red Guards broke up the Assembly.

For the next three years the Bolshevik regime fought for survival. The war with Germany was brought to a close in March 1918 when the Bolsheviks accepted the draconian terms of the Treaty of Brest-Litovsk (whereby they were forced to surrender Estonia, Latvia, Lithuania and the Russian part of Poland to Germany and Austria, and to recognize the independence of the Ukraine, Georgia and Finland), but it took until the beginning of 1920 before the Bolshevik Red Army had seen off the worst of the military challenge by the White armies led by former Tsarist officers and actively supported by Great Britain, France, the United States and Japan. By 1921, when a peace treaty was concluded with Poland following a year-long war, the survival of the Bolshevik regime was assured, and at the end of 1922 the Red Army finally took control of Vladivostok, the last stronghold of the Whites.

THE SOVIET REGIME—GORBACHEV'S INHERITANCE

Russia was renamed the Russian Soviet Federated Socialist Republic in 1918, with Moscow reinstated as the capital, and this became part of the Union of Soviet Socialist Republics in December 1922 following the consolidation of Soviet power in the Ukraine, Transcaucasia and Central Asia. The Bolshevik party was renamed the Russian Communist Party (Bolsheviks) in 1918, the

All-Union Communist Party (Bolsheviks) in 1925, and the Communist Party of the Soviet Union (CPSU) in 1952.

During the period of civil war the Bolshevik government pursued a policy of "war communism", whereby economic administration was highly centralized, all private and public wealth and manpower conscripted, private trade banned and grain and other foodstuffs forcibly requisitioned from the peasantry. This policy, which was essentially an ad hoc response to the exigencies of the military threat, had the effect of progressively distancing workers and peasants from the regime. Manifestations of popular opposition culminated in March 1921 with a mutiny at the Kronstadt naval garrison outside Petrograd. Recognizing the need to re-establish popular support for the regime, particularly among the peasantry, as well as to restore Russia's ruined industrial base, Lenin introduced the New Economic Policy (NEP) at the 10th party congress in 1921. At the outset this was limited to abandoning the system of forcible requisitioning of the peasant's produce in favour of a tax-in-kind on surpluses, but it grew to represent a much more general retreat from the principles of a socially-owned economy towards what Lenin termed "state capitalism". This combined state ownership of the "commanding heights" of the economy—heavy industry, public utilities and the financial system—with a free market and private ownership of small-scale industry and agriculture.

Lenin died in January 1924. By this time the party leadership had divided into four factions: a leftist group led by Leon Trotsky; a faction surrounding Yosef Stalin; the "Leningrad group" led by Grigory Zinoviev and Lev Kamenev, and a moderate group led by Nikolai Bukharin, Alexei Rykov (who succeeded Lenin as Prime Minister) and Mikhail Tomsky. Zinoviev and Kamenev allied with Stalin to ensure that Trotsky did not succeed Lenin as leader, and were instrumental in convincing the party central committee to ignore a recommendation made by Lenin shortly before his death that Stalin should be removed from the post of party general secretary. Lenin was concerned at the dangers posed by the unlimited authority Stalin had accumulated since his appointment in 1922. However, Zinoviev and Kamenev broke with Stalin in 1925, fearing his growing power, and in the following year they formed the "united opposition" with Trotsky, while Stalin allied with Bukharin's faction. The 15th party congress in 1927 expelled Trotsky, Zinoviev, Kamenev and 74 of their leading supporters from the party, and while many of them, including Zinoviev and Kamenev, were subsequently readmitted, Trotsky was forced into exile in 1929.

The factional struggle largely turned on economic issues. Trotsky and the left advocated a policy of accelerated industrialization, financed at the expense of the peasantry, whereas Bukharin, who was initially supported by

Stalin, favoured conciliation of the peasantry, who were to be encouraged to form co-operatives voluntarily. After the defeat of the left opposition in 1927, however, Stalin turned against the "right deviation" and eventually secured the expulsion from the politburo of Bukharin, Rykov and Tomsky in November 1929 and their replacement by his own supporters. At the beginning of 1928 Stalin signalled the end of the NEP when he launched a policy of rapid industrialization under the first five-year plan, and at the end of the following year full collectivization of agriculture was announced.

The desirability of voluntary collectivization had been proclaimed at the 15th party congress in December 1927. However, a growing crisis over the withholding of grain supplies by the kulaks (the richest class of peasant farmers who were generally hostile to government plans for agriculture) prompted a government terror campaign in the countryside in 1929–30. The kulaks were effectively "liquidated" as a class, either being executed or banished to remote areas, and a programme of forcing the rest of the peasantry into collective farms was begun. These measures met with fierce resistance and caused massive disruption to agriculture, including a widespread famine in 1932–33.

During the 17th party congress in January 1934 suggestions were put forward that Stalin should be replaced by Sergei Kirov, who had succeeded Zinoviev as secretary of the party committee in Leningrad. In December of that year Kirov was assassinated, probably on Stalin's orders, and his death was made the pretext for a reign of terror which reached its height in 1936–38. It is estimated that half a million people were executed and millions more imprisoned in forced labour camps, most of them without trial. Many of those executed were party members, including the majority of the central committee elected in 1934, and at show trials Stalin's former opponents in the leadership, including Zinoviev, Kamenev, Bukharin and Rykov, were condemned to death after making obviously false confessions of treason and terrorism. Trotsky was also sentenced to death in absentia, and was murdered by a Soviet agent in Mexico in 1940. Severe political repressions lasted until Stalin's death in 1953.

After unsuccessful attempts to form an alliance with Great Britain and France, the Soviet Union signed a non-aggression pact with Nazi Germany in August 1939. This included secret protocols dividing Eastern Europe into German and Soviet spheres of influence, and provided the pretext for the Soviet annexation of eastern Poland one month later, and of Estonia, Latvia, Lithuania and the Romanian territories of Bukovina and Bessarabia in June 1940. However, on June 22, 1941, the German army invaded the Soviet Union, capturing vast territories and inflicting massive human and material damage in the European part of the country. The German armies were finally expelled from the Soviet Union after a struggle in which about 20 million Soviet citizens lost their lives.

Upon Stalin's death in March 1953 a collective leadership was established, headed by Georgy Malenkov, who succeeded Stalin as both Prime Minister and party first secretary (the title of general secretary being abolished), Foreign Minister Vyacheslav Molotov and Lavrenti Beria, the notorious head of the secret police. Malenkov was forced to relinquish the party leadership to Nikita Khrushchev after little more than a week, however, while Beria was expelled from the party in July of that year and was subsequently executed for treason; Malenkov also relinquished the premiership in 1955 to Nikolai Bulganin. At the 20th party congress in February 1956 Khrushchev bitterly attacked Stalin's dictatorial methods, his use of terrorism and the personality cult surrounding him. In the following year Malenkov, Molotov and Lazar Kaganovich attempted to depose Khrushchev, whereupon they were accused of setting up an "anti-party group" and were expelled from the central committee. In 1958 Khrushchev also assumed the office of Prime Minister. The 22nd party congress in 1961, at which Khrushchev intensified his criticism of Stalin and the "anti-party group", adopted a new party programme and party rules, which condemned the personality cult, provided for periodic renewal of leading bodies and affirmed the right of members to criticize the leadership, while maintaining the ban on factionalism.

Strong opposition was aroused by Khrushchev's erratic domestic policies, which included unworkable overhauls of regional administration and central economic planning, and by his conduct of international relations. In October 1964 his critics in the leadership brought about his replacement as first secretary (later general secretary) by Leonid Brezhnev and as Prime Minister by Alexei Kosygin. The new leadership largely reversed Khrushchev's comparatively liberal policies and carried out a limited rehabilitation of Stalin; moreover, after the invasion of Czechoslovakia in 1968 the so-called Brezhnev Doctrine enunciated the right of the Soviet Union to intervene in socialist countries where there was a danger of socialism being overturned. In 1977, Brezhnev became head of state when he assumed the post of President of the Presidium of the Supreme Soviet. Kosygin was succeeded as Prime Minister in 1980 by Nikolai Tikhonov.

Brezhnev died in November 1982, aged 75, whereupon Yury Andropov succeeded him both as party general secretary and head of state. Andropov began cautious economic reforms and a major anti-corruption campaign, and began to remove leading officials associated with Brezhnev, but he fell seriously ill after less than a year in office and died in February 1984, at the age of 69. He was succeeded in both posts by Konstantin Chernenko, a conservative protegé of Brezhnev. In the 13 months until Chernenko's death in March 1985, aged 73, Andropov's limited reforms were continued, but at a more cautious pace and without any major new initiatives.

CHRONOLOGY

878   Establishment of Kiev as capital of Slav federation known as Kievan Rus by Oleg, chieftain of the Varangians.

988   Conversion of Kievan Rus to Orthodox Christianity by Byzantine monks during reign of Grand Prince Vladimir (978–1015)

1237–1240   Tatar invasion. Beginning of two centuries of Russian subjugation to Tatar overlordship.

1380   Russian victory at Battle of Kulikovo Polye. Beginning of struggle to throw off Tatar overlordship culminating in cessation of Russian payment of tribute c. 1480.

1462–1505   Reign of Grand Prince Ivan III of Muscovy. Consolidation of independent Russian domains under Muscovite rule.

1533–1584   Reign of Ivan IV ("The Terrible"), first Tsar of all the Russias. Eastward expansion begun with capture of Tatar khanates of Kazan (1552) and Astrakhan (1556).

1696–1725   Reign of Peter I ("The Great"). Victory in war against Sweden (1700–21) results in annexation of Estonia, Livonia (northern Latvia) and the lands around the head of the Gulf of Finland, where St Petersburg established as new capital in 1703.

1762–1796   Reign of Catherine II ("The Great"). Partitions of Poland (1772, 1793 and 1795) allow Russian incorporation of western Ukraine, Byelorussia and Courland (Lithuania and southern Latvia); peace treaties with Ottoman Turks (1774 and 1792) allow annexation of lands south to the Black Sea.

1801   Incorporation of Georgia.

1809 Annexation of Finland from Sweden.

1812–1814 Invasion by Napolean's armies followed by Russian military campaign through Europe.

1825 Failed *coup d'état* by Decembrists.

1853–1856 Crimean War against Turkey, Great Britain and France ends in Russian defeat.

1861 Emancipation of the serfs.

1872 Publication of first volume of Marx's *Das Kapital* in Russian translation.

1881 Assassination of Alexander II.

March 1898 First Congress of the Russian Social Democratic Labour Party in Minsk.

1903 Division of Russian Social Democratic Labour Party into Bolshevik and Menshevik factions.

1904–1905 Russian defeat in war with Japan coincides with nationwide insurrection, during which revolutionary soviets (councils) of workers' deputies appear for the first time. Tsar Nicholas II consents to the formation of a parliament, the *Duma*.

1912 Establishment of independent Bolshevik party.

August 1914 Russian entry into First World War against Central Powers.

March 1917 Spontaneous demonstrations and strikes in Petrograd (St Petersburg) supported by troops. Tsar Nicholas II forced to abdicate and provisional government established.

Nov. 7, 1917 Bolsheviks seize power in coup d'état against provisional government.

Jan. 18–19, 1918   Meeting of Constituent Assembly, elected in November 1917 with Bolsheviks in the minority, broken up by Bolshevik Red Guards.

March 1918   Treaty of Brest-Litovsk ends war with Germany.

July 10, 1918   Adoption of first Constitution of Russian Soviet Federal Socialist Republic by fifth All-Russian Congress of Soviets.

July 18, 1918   Murder of Nicholas II and his family by their Bolshevik captors at Ekaterinburg.

1918–1920   Civil war between Bolshevik Red Army and White armies led by former Tsarist officers and actively supported by Great Britain, France, the United States and Japan.

1920–21   War with Poland.

March 1921   Revolt of naval garrison at Kronstadt brings about end of "war communism" and ushers in New Economic Policy announced at 10th party congress.

December 1922   Creation of Union of Soviet Socialist Republics.

Jan. 21, 1924   Death of Vladimir Ilich Lenin.

1928   Abandonment of New Economic Policy and beginning of first five-year plan.

1929–30   Forced collectivization of agriculture begins.

Dec. 5, 1936   Adoption of second Soviet Constitution.

August 1939   Signature of non-aggression pact with Nazi Germany, including secret protocols providing for partition of Eastern Europe.

September 1939   Annexation of eastern Poland.

1939–1940   Winter war with Finland.

June 1940 Annexation of Lithuania, Latvia, Estonia and territories from Romania.

June 22, 1941 Nazi Germany invades the Soviet Union.

May 8, 1945 Victory in Europe follows fall of Berlin to Soviet Red Army.

March 5, 1953 Death of Stalin. Succeeded as CPSU first secretary by Nikita Khrushchev following brief power struggle within leadership.

Feb. 24–25, 1956 Khrushchev denounces Stalin at secret session of 20th CPSU congress.

Nov. 4, 1956 Soviet military intervention to suppress anti-Communist uprising in Hungary.

1957 Malenkov, Molotov and Kaganovich expelled from CPSU leadership for attempting to depose Khrushchev.

Oct. 15, 1964 Khrushchev forced to resign by opponents in the party leadership. Replaced as CPSU first secretary by Leonid Brezhnev and as Prime Minister by Alexei Kosygin.

Aug. 20, 1968 Soviet-led Warsaw Pact invasion of Czechoslovakia.

1977 Adoption of third Soviet Constitution.

Dec. 25–26, 1979 Beginning of Soviet military intervention in Afghanistan.

Nov. 10–12, 1982 Death of Brezhnev and accession of Yury Andropov as general secretary of CPSU.

Feb. 9–13, 1984 Death of Andropov and accession of Konstantin Chernenko as CPSU general secretary.

March 10–11, 1985 Death of Chernenko and accession of Mikhail Gorbachev as CPSU general secretary.

N.B. The Julian calendar was used in Russia until February 1918, by which time it had fallen 13 days behind the Gregorian calendar which was adopted in its place to bring Russia into line with the West. Therefore, what are commonly referred to as the February and October revolutions of 1917 occurred in March and November according to the modern calendar.

CHANGING THE GUARD: GORBACHEV TAKES POWER

At an extraordinary plenary meeting on March 11, 1985, the day after Chernenko's death, the CPSU central committee elected Mikhail Gorbachev as the new party general secretary. Gorbachev's candidature had been sponsored by the veteran Foreign Minister, Andrei Gromyko, and was reportedly endorsed unanimously. At 54 the youngest member of the central committee politburo, Gorbachev's election brought the Soviet Union a comparatively youthful, energetic and dynamic leader after more than a decade of ailing gerontocracy.

Mikhail Gorbachev was born on March 2, 1931, the son of a peasant farmer, in the village of Privolnoye in Stavropol *Kray* (territory) in the northern Caucasus. After working as a tractor driver in his home area, he studied law at Moscow University, graduating in 1955. Having joined the CPSU in Moscow in 1952, he returned to his home region to work as a Komsomol (Communist Youth Union) official, becoming first secretary of that organization in Stavropol city in 1956, and then successively second and first Komsomol secretary of the region. In 1962 he began working as a regional CPSU official with responsibility for collective and state farms, becoming first secretary of the party committee in Stavropol city in 1966, and second secretary for the Stavropol territory in 1968. During this period he had also completed a correspondence course in agricultural studies, which together with his law degree made him the most educated Soviet leader since Lenin.

Gorbachev was appointed first secretary of the CPSU committee in Stavropol *Kray* in 1970, and was elected a full member of the CPSU central committee in the following year. In November 1978 he was called to Moscow to join the central committee secretariat, taking over the responsibilities for agriculture made vacant by the sudden death of Fyodor Kulakov in the previous

July. Kulakov had been the first secretary of the party committee in Stavropol *Kray* in 1960–64, and was thought to have been instrumental in Gorbachev's advance in the party hierarchy in the years up to 1971. Gorbachev's promotion to Moscow, his election as a candidate member of the politburo in November 1979 and as a full politburo member in October 1980 were assumed by Western analysts to reflect the influence of Mikhail Suslov, then a prominent member of the politburo and secretariat, who had been party leader in Stavropol *Kray* during the war.

Following the election of Andropov (also a native of the northern Caucasus) as Party general secretary of the CPSU in November 1982, Gorbachev became closely identified with the new leader's campaign for greater discipline and efficiency and with his economic experiments, and he assisted in the process of replacing party officials in the regions and in the central committee departments. During this period he came to be seen as the likely successor to the leadership, and was believed to have opposed Chernenko's election. Nevertheless, during Chernenko's term as party general secretary, and partly as a result of the latter's increasing incapacity through ill health, Gorbachev continued to grow more prominent, while the scope of his responsibilities widened to include ideology, foreign affairs, party cadre appointments and overall economic policy.

Gorbachev's succession was the swiftest in Soviet history following the death of a leader since Stalin took over from Lenin in 1924. The speed with which the announcement was made, so shortly after news of Chernenko's death had been released, led observers to conclude that the succession had been agreed within the politburo some time earlier and that the central committee had been summoned to Moscow before Chernenko's death. Furthermore, Soviet newspapers of March 12 broke with tradition by printing Gorbachev's portrait on the front page and Chernenko's on page two.

Apart from a vacancy caused by the death of Marshal Dmitry Ustinov, the Defence Minister, there had been no changes in the composition of the politburo during Chernenko's 13 months in office, and although some younger members had previously been brought in by Andropov, about half of the remainder were old Brezhnevites who might be expected to have reservations about Gorbachev's leadership, particularly since his commitment to reform was made clear from the outset. At the next central committee plenum on April 23, Gorbachev brought into the politburo fellow Andropov protegés Yegor Ligachev and Nikolai Ryzhkov, who were already members of the secretariat (responsible for cadre policy and the economy, respectively). In a departure from normal practice, they were brought in directly as voting members (i.e. without a customary period as a "candidate", or non-voting, member). Also joining them as a full politburo member was Viktor Chebrikov, Andropov's appointee as chairman of the KGB and a former candidate member. The military's position in the party hierarchy was downgraded when Ustinov's successor as Defence Minister, Marshal Sergei Solokov, was admitted to the politburo as a candidate member only.

Gorbachev moved swiftly to consolidate his position. The resignation of Grigory Romanov from the politburo and secretariat at the next central committee plenum on July 1, ostensibly "on health grounds", was widely interpreted as a move engineered by Gorbachev to remove a leading opponent. It followed rumours that Romanov, the party secretary responsible for defence industries and former Leningrad party leader, had challenged Gorbachev for the succession to Chernenko, possibly with the backing of the Moscow city party leader and politburo member, Viktor Grishin. Romanov (whose removal was preceded by widespread, and possibly officially inspired, rumours of alcoholism) was replaced in the secretariat by Lev Zaikov (previously his successor in Leningrad), while Boris Yeltsin was also brought into the secretariat.

The same plenum saw the elevation to full politburo membership of Eduard Shevardnadze, first secretary of the Georgian party. On the following day, at a meeting of the Supreme Soviet, Shevardnadze was appointed Foreign Minister in place of Gromyko, who was elected Chairman of the Supreme Soviet Presidium (i.e. head of state), an office left vacant since Chernenko's death. These appointments took many people by surprise, first because Shevardnadze was thought to be lacking in foreign affairs experience, and secondly because it had been assumed that, like his three predecessors, Gorbachev would himself assume the office of head of state. Nevertheless, the astuteness of the move was impressive: by elevating Shevardnadze, an associate from the Stavropol days and now a trusted ally, Gorbachev both enhanced his own position in the politburo and stood to acquire closer control over the direction of foreign policy. Gromyko, meanwhile, suffered a diminution of political influence, but retained his membership of the politburo (and thus his involvement in the broad field of decision making) while also acquiring an office which carried high formal prestige and status.

The fact that the main evening television news on July 1, scheduled to be extended to include a summary of Gorbachev's speech to the central committee plenum, was curtailed, and that the speech was not published in the next day's press, appeared to lend credence to unofficial reports that there had been a heated argument between Gorbachev and Nikolai Tikhonov, the Chairman of the Council of Ministers (Prime Minister), who was being cast in the role of leader of the residual Brezhnevite faction within the politburo. On Sept. 27, Tikhonov resigned as Chairman, again ostensibly "for health reasons" and Ryzhkov was named as his successor. At the next central committee plenum on Oct. 16, Tikhonov was routinely dropped from the politburo, and Ryzhkov left the secretariat.

Before the end of Gorbachev's first year in office, the removal of one of his key opponents, Viktor Grishin, was made inevitable by the gradual erosion of his Moscow power base. Towards the end of 1985, the press repeatedly criticized the conduct of the capital's administration, and in mid-November Vasily Konotop was replaced as first secretary in Moscow *oblast* (region) by Valentin Mesyats, Minister of Agriculture since 1976 and thus well known to Gorbachev. Then on Dec. 24, Grishin was removed from the influential office of party first secretary in Moscow city at a meeting attended by Gorbachev, and Yeltsin was named as his replacement (the official announcement made no mention of thanks for Grishin's services, usually an indication of disfavour). Thereafter, Grishin's removal from the politburo was a foregone conclusion, and was brought about at the next central committee plenum on Feb. 18, 1986. On the same day, Yeltsin was named as a candidate politburo member, although he left the secretariat to concentrate on cleaning up the Moscow administration.

Gorbachev's first year in office also witnessed an enormous turnover of personnel at the top of ministries, in the regional party administrations, and in the republics. The changes were most marked in ministries dealing with economic affairs, where officials appointed under Brezhnev were replaced by personnel of Gorbachev's own generation who shared his enthusiasm for reform.

The 27th congress of the CPSU, held in Moscow from Feb. 25 to March 6, 1986, was an important milestone in Gorbachev's reform campaigns. The congress debated and endorsed extensive reports by Gorbachev and Ryzhkov setting out the goals of *perestroika* ("restructuring") in the economy and in Soviet society (see subsequent chapter), and adopted a revised version of the third CPSU programme and the party statutes adopted under Khrushchev in 1961. At the close of the congress, the nearly 5,000 party delegates elected a new central committee consisting of 307 full members and 170 candidate members, in which more than 40 per cent of the members were replaced.

Gorbachev's position was strengthened still further when the new central committee elected more of his supporters to the politburo and secretariat, although leading Brezhnevites like Dinmukhamed Kunayev and Vladimir Shcherbitsky were still to be found in the politburo. Zaikov became a full politburo member, while Nikolai Slyunkov (the first secretary of the Byelorussian CP) and Yury Soloviev (Zaikov's successor in July 1985 as part first secretary in Leningrad *oblast*) were elected as candidate members in place of Vasily Kuznetsov and Boris Ponomaryov. Extensive changes took place in the secretariat, with five new members being brought in, including Aleksandra Biryukova, the first woman to hold senior party office since the early 1960s.

Although Gorbachev now appeared to be strongly supported within the uppermost ranks of the Party, conservative resistance still remained strong within the central committee (where the high turnover of members at the congress had nevertheless left many members of the old guard in place), and was believed to be even more firmly entrenched in the middle ranks of the party apparatus and in the state bureaucracy. The strength of this resistance resulted in a series of unprecedented delays to a central committee plenum on cadre policy planned to take place before the end of 1986. The CPSU statutes required that plenums should take place at least every six months, but after a plenum in mid-June the meeting devoted to cadre policy was postponed three times and finally convened only on Jan. 27, 1987.

In a speech to this plenum Gorbachev announced that the stagnation which had overtaken the country's economic, social and spiritual development was the fault of the party leadership, within which conservatism, inertia, and procrastination had come to prevail. The role of party meetings and elective bodies had weakened progressively and "authoritarian evaluations and opinions became unquestionable truths". Gorbachev complained that many senior party officials had been beyond control or criticism, and abuses of authoriy had in some cases involved overtly criminal activity. In order to restore Lenin's principle of democratic centralism and accountabilty of officials, Gorbachev announced an initiative for the extension of democracy and electoral reform, observing: "A house can be put in order only by someone who feels he owns the house".

The plenum elected Aleksandr Yakovlev, currently propaganda secretary and one of Gorbachev's closest associates, as a candidate politburo member. Furthermore, Kunayev was finally removed from the politburo, a foregone conclusion since his "retirement" as first secretary of the Kazakh CP in the previous December. The removal of Kunayev from the leadership of his home republic had been expected for some time in the light of persistent reports in the official media exposing corruption and incompetence extending to the highest levels of the Kazakh administration. However, the appointment of a Russian, Gennady Kolbin, to replace Kunayev provoked an outbreak of nationalist rioting by students in the Kazakh capital, Alma Ata, on Dec. 17–18, during which, according to unofficial reports, local party officials had deliberately done nothing to contain the violence. Kunayev was one of numerous lofty figures, very many of them in Soviet Central Asia, who fell foul of the anti-corruption campaign inherited from Andropov and stepped up considerably under Gorbachev. This process brought to light cases of large-scale institutional corruption, black marketeering and abuses of official status, leading to lengthy prison sentences or even execution for offenders and dismissals of officials in the central government, and in republican and regional administrations. Ousting corrupt and incompetent officials was crucial for the success of Gorbachev's policies, since large numbers of these functionaries were ensconced in powerful positions in the middle ranks, and, desperate to preserve their status and privileges, they represented a dangerous potential opposition force which needed to be outflanked.

A principal weapon in the anti-corruption campaign was the policy known as *glasnost* ("openness"), which encouraged open discussion and criticism among officials and in the media of topics hitherto taboo in Soviet public life (see also pp.37-39). It was through the increasingly bold revelations in the official press and in the outspoken criticisms heard from the platforms of official meetings that the condemnation of corruption and the other ills which had flourished during Brezhnev's rule (initially only referred to euphemistically as the "period of stagnation") evolved in the course of 1986 and 1987 into an explicit vilification of Brezhnev himself. This reached a symbolic climax at the end of 1988 with the sentencing to 12 years in prison of Brezhnev's son-in-law, Yury Churbanov, for taking bribes worth more than a million US dollars.

At the end of May 1987 Gorbachev was presented with a golden opportunity to strengthen party control over the military establishment, which had been considered one of the main bastions of resistance to his policies, particularly his international arms control initiatives and his plans to curtail spending on armaments manufacture. On May 28 a young West German amateur pilot, Mathias Rust, made an unauthorized and unimpeded flight in a light aircraft from Helsinki in Finland across Estonia and north-western Russia to the centre of Moscow, where he landed beside the walls of the Kremlin close to Red Square. This astonishing breach of Soviet air defences (made still more embarrassing in view of the fact that May 28 was celebrated annually in the Soviet Union as Border Guards' day) prompted the sacking of a number of senior officers, including the Commander-in-Chief of the air defence forces, Marshal Aleksandr Koldunov, and Marshal Sokolov, the Defence Minister.

Sokolov's successor, Gen. Dmitry Yazov, took over his seat in the politburo at the next central committee plenum in June 1987. Three other key Gorbachev allies were also elevated to full politburo membership—Slyunkov, Nikonov and Yakovlev.

Towards the end of 1987 Gorbachev suffered what appeared to be a setback with the sacking of Yeltsin as party leader in Moscow and his subsequent removal from the politburo. Yeltsin, hitherto regarded as one of the keenest supporters of Gorbachev's reforms, had become known for his radicalism and for outspoken attacks on conservatism and bureaucracy. At a central committee plenum on Oct. 21 he made a strongly worded attack on other senior members of the leadership whom he accused of frustrating reform; he also reportedly criticized aspects of the present leadership style, including, apparently, the high profile of Gorbachev's wife Raisa. Reports of Yeltsin's outburst, which was not officially acknowledged in the Soviet media until some considerable time after the event, indicated that he had traded insults with politburo colleagues, notably Ligachev, who as party secretary for ideology was assumed to be the most senior member of the leadership after Gorbachev. With the eclipse of the Brezhnevites, Ligachev had come to be regarded as the leading conservative in the leadership because of statements urging caution and restraint in the application of reforms.

As a direct consequence of this outburst, Yeltsin was sacked from his Moscow post at a meeting of the capital's CPSU committee on Nov. 11, when speakers including Gorbachev accused him of excessive personal ambition, vanity and "serious crime against the party". Gorbachev himself rejected Yeltsin's criticisms at the October plenum and accused him of excessive haste and hectoring and of employing "pseudo-revolutionary" leadership methods. Yeltsin was replaced by Zaikov, and on Nov. 18 was named as a First Deputy Chairman of the USSR State Construction Committee, with the rank of minister—effectively a demotion.

The Oct. 21 central committee meeting had seen the retirement from the politburo of Geidar Aliyev, who also retired two days later as a First Deputy Premier. Yeltsin was routinely dropped from candidate membership of the politburo at the next central committee plenum on Feb. 18, 1988.

The same plenum also elected two other Gorbachev loyalists as candidate politburo members: Yury Maslyukov, who had taken over as Chairman of the State Planning Committee (*Gosplan*) after his predecessor, Talyzin, had been publicly criticized for failing to curtail its bureaucratic excesses, and Georgy Razumovsky, for the last two years the secretary for party organization.

Another crucial stage in the consolidation of Gorbachev's powers came at the end of June 1988 with the holding of the first extraordinary party conference since 1941. The conference had been anticipated both by political commentators and by the Soviet public as a test of the strength of Gorbachev's support within the party, and was preceded by months of intense speculation about disputes between conservative and reformist factions.

Although rumours of divisions over Gorbachev's policies had never abated since he had taken office as general secretary, a major dispute had come into the open in the middle of March when *Sovietskaya Rossiya*, the newspaper of the party and government leadership in the Russian Federation, published a reader's letter sharply criticizing Gorbachev's policies as too liberal and as a threat to Soviet socialism. There followed allegations that Ligachev had personally endorsed publication of the letter, taking advantage of Gorbachev's absence on an official visit abroad. Three weeks passed before a rejoinder appeared, during which time the original letter had been reprinted widely in provincial newspapers and had been discussed publicly as if it represented a change of official policy. Gorbachev himself later conceded publicly that "acute clashes of opinion" had caused confusion and alarm in the Soviet Union. Nevertheless, the rejoinder, published in *Pravda* and unofficially attributed to Yakovlev, was followed by an editorial in *Sovietskaya Rossiya* admitting that publication of the letter had been a mistake, and by widespread rumour that Ligachev had been officially reprimanded and forced to relinquish some of his key secretariat responsibilities to Yakovlev.

There had been further evidence of confrontation between conservatives and reformers in the course of the selection of delegates for the party conference. The selection procedure provided for nominations from party cells to be passed upwards for approval by successive strata of the party organization before a final vote in the regional party committees, but there were numerous reports that district and regional committees were rigging the selection by substituting their own chosen delegates for reformist nominees put forward by grassroots party cells. These reports led to demonstrations in several cities and to the sacking of some officials.

In his keynote speech to the opening session of the conference on June 28, Gorbachev advocated far-reaching reforms to the political system in order to make *perestroika* irreversible, characterizing these reforms as a return to Leninist principles. His proposals included a clear separation of the functions of party and government bodies, multi-candidate elections, time limits on the holding of party and government office, revival of the elected soviet as the real instrument of government at all levels, and a new structure of state and government bodies. He also called for freedom of opinion and debate and for reinstatement of the rule of law. The speeches in the debate which followed were remarkable for the candour with which opinions were voiced on a wide range of subjects, many of which would not have been open to question before Gorbachev took office, and the last day of the debate saw dramatic public recriminations between Ligachev and Yeltsin. The closing session, at which Gorbachev's proposals were endorsed, lasted several hours longer than scheduled while the delegates engaged in what was officially described as "unusually stormy and prolonged" discussion about the wording of the conference resolutions.

In the name of putting into effect conference decisions, Gorbachev further strengthened his position in the party on Sept. 30, when a central committee plenum approved a drastic reduction in the central committee apparatus. Further major changes in the leadership featured the retirement or relegation to the sidelines of most of the remaining conservatives. The plenum had been convened in haste, and some commentators suggested that Gorbachev had acted to seize an advantageous moment after receiving assurances from party "scouts" at large in the regions throughout the summer that a majority within the central committee would support his proposals for its reorganization. Others suggested that the urgent need to remove bureaucratic obstacles to economic reform had been impressed upon Gorbachev more firmly than ever during a recent tour of Siberian cities, where he had been heckled by citizens complaining that *perestroika* had failed to improve living standards and eliminate food shortages.

The leadership changes saw the removal from the politburo of Gromyko and three other Brezhnevite survivors, leaving only Shcherbitsky as representative of the old guard. Brought in to replace them were Vadim Medvedev as a full member and as candidate members Anatoly Lukyanov, Biryukova and Aleksandr Vlasov (soon to be appointed Prime Minister of the Russian Federation). The only new member was Chebrikov, who on the following day relinquished the chairmanship of the KGB to a relatively unknown career KGB officer, leaving the KGB apparently downgraded through lack of politburo representation.

The reorganization of the central committee also assigned new roles to secretariat members, who were put in charge of newly formed commissions. As a consequence, Ligachev was finally confirmed to have relinquished responsibility for ideology, with Medvedev now taking charge of the new ideology commission and Ligachev taking charge of the commission for agrarian policy. This transfer, while not technically a demotion, was widely viewed as a move which would engage Ligachev's still considerable authority in tackling the Soviet Union's most intractable problem, but at the same time would remove him from the mainstream of discussion within the leadership by burdening him with extremely demanding daily tasks.

Gorbachev finally took over the role of head of state as the result of an extraordinary session of the Supreme Soviet on Oct. 1, at which Gromyko retired. Lukyanov took over as first deputy head of state.

The conference proposals for democratization and for reorganizing state and government bodies became law on Dec. 1, 1988, when the Supreme

Soviet approved amendments to the 1977 Constitution and to the electoral law allowing for the election of a new supreme representative body, the 2,250-member Congress of People's Deputies. The Congress was in turn to elect a much smaller Supreme Soviet to serve as a standing parliament, meeting twice yearly for three- to four-month sessions, and an executive state president, to be known as the Chairman of the Supreme Soviet (a post seemingly tailor-made for Gorbachev himself).

The Congress elections were held in mid-March 1989 for 750 seats reserved for approved social organizations (including 100 for the CPSU), and, in direct popular voting on March 26, for 1500 single-member constituencies. Although the process of nominating and selecting candidates to stand in the constituency elections had presented opportunities for manipulation by the electoral commissions, two or more candidates were put forward in three quarters of the constituencies. The elections themselves produced some remarkable upsets, with a number of senior CPSU officials throughout the country being defeated by opponents from the party rank-and-file, by representatives of unofficial political groups or by independent candidates; others were denied enough votes to be elected unopposed.

Probably the most striking result was the landslide victory in Moscow for Boris Yeltsin, who was standing against a local factory director regarded as the "official" party candidate. The highest-ranking loser was candidate politburo member Soloviev, who fell victim to an unofficial opposition campaign which routed most of the Leningrad leadership. In the immediate aftermath of the elections, the Soviet newspapers were extremely circumspect in their reporting of the results, giving the impression that there was confusion as to what interpretation was to be put on the rejection of party figures by the electorate. However, in a press briefing on March 29 Gorbachev claimed that the election results had been a victory for *perestroika* and democratization, interpreting the defeat of party leaders as a criticism of their failure to change and a call for faster reform.

Gorbachev secured yet another major victory in his efforts to remove the threat of conservative opposition when a central committee plenum at the end of April 1989 approved the "retirement" of 74 of its full members and 24 candidate members, most of whom constituted the last of the old guard. Addressing a press conference after the plenum, Medvedev described this purge of "dead souls" (so called because they had already lost the offices which had entitled them to a central committee seat) as "a major landmark in the history of *perestroika*". Gorbachev claimed in the main address to the plenum that all those retiring had signed a letter requesting it "in the interests of the cause" and for reasons of age or ill health, and that "new tasks" required "a very serious regrouping of forces in the party and in society as a whole". The departing central committee members included Gromyko, along with all the old Brezhnev protégés already ousted by Gorbachev from the highest party ranks.

The Congress of People's Deputies finally convened on May 25, 1989, when Gorbachev was elected unopposed to the new executive presidency, but only after remarkably candid debate by the 2,250 Congress deputies; 87 deputies voted against him. In the course of the next two weeks, the range and openness of Congress discussions, and the excitement which they generated among ordinary Soviet people, bore further witness to the transformations which had been wrought in Soviet political life by four years of Gorbachev's leadership.

PERESTROIKA:
"IF NOT US, WHO? IF NOT NOW, WHEN?"

Gorbachev's election as CPSU leader encouraged expectations of new impetus to the efforts begun by Andropov aimed at reversing the Soviet Union's economic decline, and at dispelling the attendant malaise afflicting public morale and morality. Whereas Andropov had not had sufficient opportunity to make major policy changes in the economic sphere, and Chernenko apparently had lacked the inclination, Gorbachev, in his capacity as party secretary for agriculture after 1978, had been well placed to investigate the country's grave economic shortcomings before taking up the party leadership. In the year before he took office, Gorbachev was also believed to have sought the advice of leading Soviet economists in a series of private seminars.

In his address to the CPSU central committee following his election, Gorbachev gave the first outline of his proposals for a complete restructuring of economic activity in the Soviet Union. *Perestroika,* the Russian term meaning "restructuring", was soon to become the watchword of Gorbachev's entire programme to reform the Soviet Union.

As described by Gorbachev, economic *perestroika* would involve "switching onto a track of intensive development". This acknowledged the fact that economic growth could no longer be sustained simply by drawing additional labour and material resources into production, but would instead need technical innovation, complete retooling, automation, and more efficient use of materials and labour. Gorbachev also spoke of the need "persistently to improve the economic mechanism and the whole system of management", which would include "strengthening socialist ownership, broadening rights, enhancing the independence of enterprises, and increasing their interest in the end results of their work". Shortly afterwards, at the beginning of April 1985, Gorbachev attested to the urgency of *perestroika* when he complained that the economy was beset by lack of organization, complacency and irresponsibility, and in June he went further in publicly identifying the policies of the 1970s as the source of current economic difficulties.

In the same month, Gorbachev announced that the politburo had taken the unprecedented step of ordering the redrafting of the five-year plan for 1986–90 in order to reflect a new emphasis on renovating and re-equipping existing plant, on improving product quality, and on making centralized planning more responsive to demand.

The landmark event in the implementation of *perestroika* came just under a year after Gorbachev took office as Soviet leader, with the convening of the 27th CPSU congress at the end of February 1986.

In his keynote address, Gorbachev began by announcing that the party leadership considered it necessary "to tell the party and the people honestly and frankly about the deficiencies in our political and practical activities, the unfavourable tendencies in the economy and the social and moral sphere, and the reasons for them". Condemning the inertness of the administration under Brezhnev (albeit refraining from criticizing the late leader by name) and the "signs of stagnation" which had been allowed to develop, he announced a strategy of "acceleration" (*uskoreniye*) of the country's socio-economic development which constituted "the key to all our problems—immediate and long-term, economic and social, political and ideological, internal and external".

This was, he said, "the only way a new qualitative condition of Soviet society can and must be achieved". Not long afterwards, in a speech to a writers' conference in June, Gorbachev reiterated the gravity and urgency of this need for change when he posed the question: "If not us, who? And if not now, when?".

Following the congress, Gorbachev's specific proposals for improvements in the various sectors of the economy began to be framed in new legislation and policy directives.

In his congress speech, Gorbachev dwelt upon the need for the Soviet people to be able to appreciate material improvements within a short time, particularly in food and consumer goods supplies. However, over the next three years, the troubled agricultural and consumer sectors were to resist all the efforts of *perestroika* and stubbornly to persist as the Soviet Union's most worrying and intractable problems. Furthermore, the failure of food supplies to show any significant improvements cast doubts in the minds of many Soviet citizens about *perestroika*'s validity, and forced the leadership to embark on revolutionary changes to the collectivized system of agriculture which Stalin had forced into place more than 50 years before.

Improved planning methods and production incentives for collective and state farmers had been announced within a month of the party congress, but their effect on improving production was slight. At the beginning of 1987 Gorbachev and other party leaders publicly rebuked agricultural officials for their tardiness both in reversing the stagnation of production in this sector, and in tackling the inefficient farm management and methods of food processing and distribution which wasted 20–30 per cent of farm produce. Gorbachev complained that agriculture had been "stalled since 1972", while Ligachev illustrated the seriousness of the situation by pointing out that the Ukraine, formerly the country's "bread basket", had resorted to importing food from other areas to feed its own population.

The solution chosen by the leadership to tackle the crisis in agriculture was unveiled by Gorbachev at the extraordinary party conference in the middle of 1988. In a dramatic retreat from the principles of collectivization, Gorbachev announced that farmers should be allowed to lease land in order to "overcome the estrangement between the farmer and the soil", and that *perestroika* should "make the farmer sovereign master, protect him against command methods, and cardinally change living conditions in the countryside". A decree on leasehold arrangements for both the farming sector and other economic activities was passed in April 1989.

Outside agriculture, the new provisions for lease relations broadened the scope for private and co-operative ventures which had been developing since 1987.

Since May of that year, individuals had been permitted to engage privately on a part-time basis in certain specified activities within the production and service sectors. In approving these measures, the authorities had been forced to concede that, as one official put it, "individual labour is expedient and has to be fitted in fully with the principles of the socialist economy", and it was announced that legitimate private enterprise was needed because state and co-operative enterprises were not meeting consumer demand for goods and services. This shortcoming had meant that Soviet citizens were heavily reliant on goods and services provided on the black market, and it was estimated that between 17 and 20 million Soviet citizens (up to 15 per cent of the workforce) were engaged in some form of illegal private enterprise, almost invariably as a second job. In effect the new measures simply legalized the status quo.

The regulations for private enterprise remained restricted, however, by the prohibition on the private hiring of labour for commercial ends, and even family-run enterprises were restricted to those family members living under the same roof. On the other hand, provisions for workers' co-operatives were extended considerably in the course of 1987 and 1988.

Engaging private and co-operative enterprise, however, had little effect in solving the fundamental problems of the consumer goods sector. Indeed, by mid-1988 the recognition that the improvements in consumer goods supply promised by *perestroika* had failed to materialize, and were moreover an issue of burgeoning public dissatisfaction, appeared to be forcing the authorities towards increasingly desperate measures: in August 1988 the Council of Ministers ordered a crash programme to try to increase both supplies and quality of consumer goods, and in the latter part of the year there was also a much publicized programme to switch redundant armaments production facilities to manufacturing for the consumer goods sector. In April 1989 the government went so far as to spend 5,000 million roubles-worth of the Soviet Union's precious hard currency reserves to buy from the West clothing, footwear and toiletries.

As regards the more general issue of economic management, Gorbachev in June 1987 detailed a series of radical proposals for revitalizing the economy by drastically reducing the role of central planning and state subsidy. He told a central committee plenum called specifically to discuss *perestroika* that "taking our economy out of the pre-crisis situation in which it has found itself calls for in-depth, truly revolutionary transformations", and he stressed that the policies adopted since the introduction of *perestroika* were insignificant compared with the as yet unrealized task of forming an integrated system for managing the economy. He went on to outline a framework for reform which he termed the New Economic Mechanism, and which he hoped would be implemented in time for the start of the 13th five-year plan in 1991.

Gorbachev complained that the country had resorted to massive exports of raw materials in order to make up for the fundamental inadequacies of the rest of the economy, which had fallen badly behind the West in technological development and the efficient use of resources. He also argued that the central bodies were manifestly incapable of directing the day-to-day activities of every Soviet enterprise, and proposed that central planning should be drastically curtailed in favour of management autonomy in enterprises, which would give rise to genuine accountability of enterprises and workers, and he stressed that financial rewards should reflect more accurately individual contributions made to the economy.

The first element of the programme to devolve authority in economic planning to managers in individual enterprises was entailed in a law which entered into effect at the beginning of 1988. Enterprises were required to manage their own financial affairs on the basis of profit-and-loss accounting, rather than in accordance with centrally controlled budgets, and would bid for state contracts instead of simply complying with assignments from the centre. One result of the new law was that unprofitable enterprises hitherto propped up by state subsidies (more than one sixth of all enterprises, according to official estimates) would now face bankruptcy.

Regrettably, however, another result of devolution to enterprise managers was that some individual enterprises began to exploit chronic shortages of goods by making unwarranted price rises, while others, exercising the right to draw up their own plans, scaled down production of cheaper essential items in favour of more profitable luxury ones, thereby creating shortages where none had existed previously. Only a year after management autonomy had been introduced, these abuses forced a partial retreat with the reimposition of certain state price controls from the centre.

The progress of *perestroika* since the 1986 congress was subjected to its closest official scrutiny before the eyes of the Soviet public at the extraordinary CPSU conference held in mid-1988.

Addressing the conference, Gorbachev claimed that reforms of the economic management system were already beginning to yield positive results, but he conceded that economic revival and structural change were taking place too slowly, and that there had been little improvement in living standards. He stated that while some difficulties had arisen because most of the reforms had been introduced one or two years into the current five-year plan, they were more generally attributable to "the tenacity of managerial stereotypes". He added: "In some cases, indeed, we are running into undisguised attempts at perverting the essence of the reform, at filling new managerial forms with the old content", and he attacked enterprises which persisted in manufacturing unwanted goods for the sake of attaining meaningless gross output targets, and planning bodies for failing to adjust to supply-and-demand pressures. On wages, he criticized enterprise managements for being too timid in applying incentive schemes and for failing to eliminate levelling, stating that "the reform will not work, will not yield the results we expect, if it does not affect the personal interests of literally every individual".

He attributed the Soviet economy's sluggishness in responding to reforms to, in the main, an underestimation of "the extent and gravity of the deformations and the stagnation of the preceding period". Nevertheless, he stressed that the CPSU should be prepared to admit that better results should have been achieved in *perestroika*'s first years.

GLASNOST:
LIFTING THE LID

As well as rapid and radical changes in economic and social policy, the accession of Gorbachev marked the beginning of a period of extraordinary cultural change in the Soviet Union and moves towards much greater freedom of information and debate. Investigative journalism emerged in the official media, many books and films were unbanned, and there was greater frankness about previously taboo subjects such as social problems, disasters, and controversial aspects of Soviet history. Furthermore, the limits of public debate were extended and there was considerable relaxation in official attitudes to dissent. Such was the impact of this trend that the Russian word *glasnost* quickly entered into international usage.

The main impetus had been the need to expose economic inefficiency, bureaucratic incompetence, corruption and social ills as part of *perestroika*. Although the Soviet authorities had in the past made use of orchestrated media campaigns to expose shortcomings, the degree of self-criticism under the new style of *glasnost,* and the extent to which the media were allowed and even encouraged to take the initiative, were unprecedented.

Some commentators also portrayed *glasnost* as intended to develop greater public confidence and to encourage individual initiative by showing that incompetence and injustice were being punished, and that ordinary citizens would be protected from arbitrary penalties. On June 30, 1987, the Supreme Soviet adopted a law "On Nationwide Discussion of Important Matters of State Life" which set out procedures by which Soviet citizens, either individually or collectively, would be able to make proposals and observations on draft legislation. The first Soviet public opinion research centre was opened in March 1988.

Glasnost did not receive the unequivocal support of the party leadership, however. In mid-1987 both Ligachev and Chebrikov made statements warning that it should not be taken too far, and on several occasions *Pravda* warned journalists against overstepping the limits of *glasnost* by sensationalizing issues: criticism of failings was not a real contribution to *perestroika*, the newspaper warned, if such stories were not balanced with positive reports of the measures being taken to overcome them. Such criticism of perceived excesses in the press was renewed at the June 1988 CPSU conference, when several speakers accused newspaper editors of abusing *glasnost* deliberately to stir up factional feuding in the party and of going too far in raking up the past. However, in reply to the critics Gorbachev asserted that *"perestroika* will die if we give up advancing the process of *glasnost,* criticism, self-criticism and democracy".

A major test of the authorities' commitment to a freer information policy came with the world's worst-ever nuclear accident at the Chernobyl power station in the north Ukraine on April 26, 1986. Massive emissions of radioactive particles into the atmosphere occurred when, in the course of an unauthorized experiment by technicians, one of the station's reactors went out of control and explosions blew the roof off the building and ignited the reactor core. The emissions caused lethal contamination in areas up to 100 km from the site, and there was radioactive fallout across much of northern Europe, but initially the authorities failed to give adequate information either to the Soviet public or to neighbouring countries (the first outside information on the disaster came from Swedish monitoring). They were also slow to take vital precautionary measures, with evacuations from all but the most dangerously contaminated areas not taking place until a week after the accident.

This scandalous secrecy, a throwback to the classic Soviet response to disasters, was dramatically abandoned at the beginning of May, however, and thereafter the Chernobyl accident was covered with commendable candour and openness. Subsequently it became clear that Chernobyl had forced the Soviet authorities to reject decisively the past policy of withholding this kind of undesirable information from their own public and from the international community. Subsequent disasters, such as the earthquake in Armenia on Dec. 7, 1988, received immediate and comprehensive Soviet media coverage.

Following from the exposure of current problems and the strong official condemnation of the stagnation of the Brezhnev era, a more critical exploration of other controversial aspects of Soviet history became a feature of pronouncements by the party and government leadership, while even more forthright statements were tolerated in the press.

Gorbachev made the most significant contribution to this reappraisal of Soviet history with a speech at the beginning of November 1987 making the 70th anniversary of the October revolution. Making numerous radical departures from the previously-accepted official line he praised the "wealth of ideas" in the New Economic Policy, and called for a truthful assessment of the ideological disputes which had broken out following Lenin's death and which had allowed Stalin to take power. He attacked the "wanton repressive measures" of collectivization in the early 1930s, and the "enormous and unforgiveable" guilt of Stalin and his entourage for the repression carried out under their rule. Gorbachev announced that the process of rehabilitating innocent victims of Stalinism, started by Khrushchev, would be completed. Consequently, in the course of 1988 and early 1989, verdicts in thousands of treason trials in the Stalin era were overturned, included those of Zinoviev, Kamenev, Bukharin and Rykov.

Dramatic changes in the official attitude towards critics of the regime began in 1986 and intensified in the course of the next two years. They included the release by the end of 1988 of virtually all dissidents imprisoned for "political" offences such as "anti-Soviet agitation", a much more accommodating attitude to religious groups, and a huge increase in permitted emigration. A major review designed to "humanize" the penal code was set in motion at the beginning of 1987, and from July of that year the abuse of psychiatric treatment to incarcerate dissidents in mental hospitals was officially acknowledged and legal measures taken to bring it to an end.

By 1989 this liberalization had allowed for the formation of a plethora of informal groups, ranging from environmentalists to nationalists. Although certain of these groups engaged in activities which remained proscribed, there was increasing evidence of a generally more tolerant official attitude to public protests, and what one senior police officer described in mid-1988 as "more democratic methods with regard to the public expression of views".

NATIONALITIES:
TROUBLE IN THE FRATERNITY

One worrying side-effect of Gorbachev's reforms was the fact that in loosening the fetters on Soviet political life, they also unleashed pent-up nationalist tensions and grievances among the Soviet Union's "fraternal peoples". Even before major waves of nationalism swept the Caucasian and Baltic republics, isolated incidents such as the December 1986 Kazakhstan riots and occasional reports of tensions from various parts of the Soviet Union had prompted Gorbachev by February 1988 publicly to identify the problem of developing a correct nationalities policy as "the most fundamental and most vital issue" confronting Soviet society.

The most serious ethnic unrest ever experienced in peacetime in the Soviet Union was not, surprisingly, the consequence of separatism or anti-Russian sentiment, but rather a revival of traditional animosities between two of the Soviet Union's smaller national groups (albeit focused on a grievance dating from the imposition of Soviet rule in their republics). In February 1988, only days after Gorbachev's statement on nationalities, massive street protests and intercommunal violence erupted in the neighbouring republics of Armenia and Azerbaijan. The protests concerned the status of the autonomous *oblast* (region) of Nagorny Karabakh, which had been made part of Azerbaijan in 1921 but was populated largely by ethnic Armenians, who claimed to be the victims of cultural and economic discrimination. A constitutional crisis was precipitated on Feb. 20 when, after nearly four months of localized popular agitation and official representations to Moscow, an unprecedented vote was passed by the Nagorny Karabakh regional *soviet* to request that the region should be transferred to Armenian administration.

Demonstrations in support of the Armenians in Nagorny Karabakh began shortly afterwards in Yerevan, the Armenian capital, and within a week hundreds of thousands of people were reported to be demonstrating there daily. The personal intervention of Gorbachev secured a suspension of the protests in Yerevan at the end of February, but by then reports were emerging of incidents of intercommunal violence, by far the worst of these being horrific anti-Armenian riots on Feb. 28–29 in the Azerbaijan city of Sumgait in which 32 people were killed (the majority of them Armenians) and nearly 200 were injured. Despite hardening official attitudes to the unrest and the reinforcement of the police and militia presence with troops, intermittent mass demonstrations and strikes gripped Yerevan and Nagorny Karabakh for much of the spring and summer.

The imposition of a virtual state of emergency in Nagorny Karabakh was prompted by a flare-up of intercommunal clashes there in September, and by the end of that month troops had been deployed throughout Armenia and Azerbaijan to try to keep the peace. These did not, however, prevent renewed violence breaking out in cities in Azerbaijan at the end of November, and as a consequence of the ever-worsening tensions, Armenians were reported to be fleeing from Azerbaijan and Azerbaijanis from Armenia, in tens of thousands. One year on from the start of the Nagorny Karabakh dispute, it was officially reported to have cost the lives of 87 civilians and four soldiers, and to have forced more than 300,000 people to flee their homes.

The constitutional aspect of the Nagorny Karabakh issue caused a row between the political leaderships of Armenia and Azerbaijan, with votes in mid-June 1988 in the respective republican Supreme Soviets for and against the transfer of the disputed region, and in mid-July there was an attempt unilaterally to declare secession from Azerbaijan by the Nagorny Karabakh regional soviet. The USSR Supreme Soviet on July 18 firmly rejected the idea of transferring Nagorny Karabakh, but in January 1989, conceding that the problem was too intractable for authorities in Azerbaijan and Armenia to solve, the region was placed under "temporary" direct rule from Moscow.

Although the unrest in Armenia and Azerbaijan was serious in terms of its violence, a greater political threat to Gorbachev's policies was the nationalist agitation in the three Baltic republics of Lithuania, Latvia and Estonia. Here nationalism took a form much more recognizable to proponents of the theory that, without firm restraint from Moscow, the peoples along the fringes of the Soviet Union would clamour for self-determination.

The Baltic republics in 1988 witnessed a coalescence of the goals of unofficial nationalist agitation with official initiatives for greater autonomy. First set out prior to the extraordinary CPSU conference in June, these advocated rights for all 15 Soviet republics to determine economic policy without interference from central planning bodies in Moscow, to control immigration from other republics, and to curtail the use of Russian in official matters in preference to the local language. The issue of uncontrolled immigration was especially sensitive in Estonia and Latvia, where the native populations faced the prospect of soon becoming a minority in their own republics.

In October 1988 the authorities allowed the establishment in all three Baltic Republics of independent movements which combined support for Gorbachev's reforms with radical autonomy programmes and proposals for political pluralism; in Estonia and Latvia the founding congresses of these movements were addressed by the republican state and party leaders. Known in Estonia and Latvia as the Popular Front and in Lithuania as the Restructuring Movement or *Sajudis,* these movements turned the March 1989 constituency elections to the Congress of People's Deputies into the nearest thing to a multi-party contest ever seen in the Soviet Union by openly fielding candidates, and in all three republics they won a large share of the seats.

The Estonian Supreme Soviet voted overwhelmingly on Nov. 16, 1988, to declare the republic "sovereign". It also decided that laws passed by the USSR Supreme Soviet were effectively subject to approval by the Estonian Supreme Soviet, and it voted to transfer control over most economic resources to the republic and to legitimize private property. On the following day, however, the Presidium of the USSR Supreme Soviet pronounced the Estonian sovereignty vote to be in contravention of the Soviet constitution, while Gorbachev on Nov. 26 accused the Estonian Supreme Soviet of "political adventurism" and gave an explicit warning that excessive nationalist demands could jeopardize his reform programme. The Lithuanian and Latvian Supreme Soviets, meeting shortly after the Estonian declaration, decided to postpone voting on their own similar sovereignty declarations.

The Estonian Supreme Soviet in mid-January 1989 gave Estonian the legal status of state language (to be used for "internal official work in all institutions and at enterprises", and for legal proceedings). The following month, on Feb. 24, the anniversary of the formation in 1918 of an independent Estonian republic was officially celebrated with a public holiday and mass rally in Tallinn (the capital), during which the flag of the independent republic, restored to official status in July 1988, was hoisted above government buildings in place of the red flag of Soviet Estonia. Similarly, at the end of January the Presidium of the Lithuanian Supreme Soviet also passed a decree officially designating Lithuanian as the republican state language, and declared Feb. 16 a holiday in the republic to mark Lithuania's 1918 Act of Independence. Unofficial attempts to commemorate the anniversary in 1988 had been met with a heavy police presence and arrests.

On Aug. 23, 1988, mass rallies were held in Lithuania, Latvia and

Estonia to mark the anniversary of the 1939 Nazi-Soviet pact which had led to their incorporation into the Soviet Union. Only a year previously small-scale unofficial rallies marking the anniversary, while relatively free of police interference, had been officially denounced as Western-inspired provocations.

The issue of official status for the local language also surfaced at the beginning of 1989 in Moldavia, which like the Baltic republics, had been annexed by the Soviet Union in accordance with the 1939 Nazi-Soviet pact. This issue prompted large demonstrations in the Moldavian capital, Kishinev, in January and February, as well as smaller street protests and student sit-ins outside government buildings.

The case of the Crimean Tatars represented another nationality problem with its roots in the Second World War, but one which, by virtue of this group's relatively few numbers proved possible largely to ignore without serious worries about violence or political destabilization.

In 1944 the Crimean Tatars, along with half-a-dozen other small national groups which had found themselves under Nazi German occupation, had been accused en masse by Stalin of collaborating with the occupiers, and were forcibly deported from their homelands and dispersed in Siberia and Central Asia. The Soviet German-speaking population, with their own autonomous republic on the lower Volga river, suffered a similar fate. By the 1960s all the deported groups had been rehabilitated politically, and all had been allowed to resettle in their home areas except the Crimean Tatars, the Meskhetians of Georgia and the Volga Germans.

Crimean Tatars in the second half of 1987 held a series of peaceful demonstrations in Moscow, the Crimea and Uzbekistan (where the majority of them now lived) to press for permission to return to their homeland. They went further in urging the restoration of the Crimea as their own autonomous republic, thereby returning to them the status enjoyed by most other ethnic groups of similar numbers. As the result of a day-long sit-in by demonstrators outside the Kremlin in late July they secured the establishment of a special high-level commission to examine their case, but when this presented its findings after nearly a year's consideration it announced that the Crimea's post-war repopulation by Russians and Ukrainians made the demand for its reconstitution as the official Crimean Tatar homeland impossible, and that Crimean Tatars would be allowed to return there to live only insofar as any Soviet citizen might change his place of residence. There were no reports of a co-ordinated Crimean Tatar protest in response to the ruling.

An isolated Meskhetian protest in support of demands for their return to Georgia was reported in June 1988. By contrast, representatives of the Soviet

German-speaking population were reported in October 1988 to be engaged in official negotiations for the designation of a new autonomous region, probably to be centred on one of the areas where they had been placed following their deportation from their now defunct autonomous republic on the Volga.

It was the turn of the republic of Georgia to witness an outbreak of nationalist protest, this time featuring overtly separatist demands, at the end of 1988 and in the early months of 1989. A sudden upsurge in these protests in April 1989 was triggered, ironically, by a resurgence of demands for secession from Georgia by Abkhazians, a small national group with their own autonomous republic at the northern end of Georgia's Black Sea coast. Demonstrations on the streets of the Georgian capital, Tbilisi, culminated on April 9 in a brutal police action against a peaceful crowd of around 10,000 people, during which at least 16 were either clubbed to death or were killed by what was later revealed to have been poisonous gas. Such a show of force had not been seen since 1962, when police had gunned down participants in a workers' protest in the Russian town of Novocherkassk. There were suggestions that it had been deliberately ordered by hardliners in the Georgian administration to embarrass Gorbachev in advance of the April 25 central committee plenum, given that news of the planned clear-out of the last of the old guard had probably been circulated in advance.

Gorbachev's statement on nationalities in February 1988 had been made in support of a proposal that the central committee should devote a plenum to the nationalities problem. More than a year later that plenum had still not convened, but in the meantime the authorities had been made even more acutely aware that the realistic threat of large-scale nationalist outbreaks was not to the integrity of the Soviet Union, but to the continuation of the political reform which had allowed nationalism to find expression. They faced the dilemma of how to handle nationalism without either discrediting the reforms through resorting to the old-style repressions, or else losing control and giving ammunition to the reforms' opponents.

EASTERN EUROPE: CRACKS IN THE BLOC

In their various responses to the Soviet initiatives for change, the Soviet Union's allies in Eastern Europe revealed differences of opinion over ideology and policy to a degree which had never before found such widespread expression. In the past, the audacity of individual states to reject the Soviet line had led to the hiatuses of Yugoslavia's breakaway in 1948, Hungary's crushed revolt of 1956, Albania's withdrawal into isolation in 1961 and Czechoslovakia's suppressed "Prague Spring" of 1968, but in all cases the other states in the bloc had simply closed ranks behind the Soviet position. With the arrival of Gorbachev, however, the majority of these states dared, for a variety of reasons, to take a line openly independent of the new Soviet interpretations.

The Soviet reforms were greeted most enthusiastically in **Hungary,** whose own reform processes dating from the late 1960s had partly served Gorbachev as a model for *perestroika* in the economy. The arrival of a reformist and comparatively liberal Soviet leadership meant the release of the brakes which had been applied to Hungary's economic reform in the early 1970s at the insistence of the Brezhnev leadership. It allowed Hungary to press ahead with the more radical reforms, political and economic, which its rulers decided were necessary to overcome the state of grave economic crisis which had overtaken the country by the mid-1980s.

By the beginning of 1989, Hungary's leaders were talking openly of introducing a multi-party political system, and of holding completely free parliamentary elections by the mid-1990s. Moreover, a measure of the triumph of *glasnost* in Hungary was the disclosure in January 1989 by a senior member of the leadership that the 1956 Hungarian uprising was being officially reappraised not as a "counter-revolution" but as "a popular uprising . . . against an oligarchic system of power which had humiliated the nation".

For the authorities in **Poland,** the end of the "Brezhnev doctrine" authorizing Soviet interference in other socialist countries gave them considerably more room for manoeuvre as they sought to resolve the crisis of national confidence brought about by martial law in 1981–83 and the banning of the Solidarity free trade union. The crises in the economy and in society forced the authorities to begin a dialogue with its opponents, which by early 1989 produced reforms second only to Hungary's in the extent to which they dismantled the old political order.

Glasnost also allowed for official discussion of the many controversial matters in Polish-Soviet history, notably the massacre in 1940 of Polish officers at Katyn forest in the Soviet Union. For the first time the Polish authorities in 1989 felt able publicly to acknowledge Soviet culpability for a crime which Poles regarded as a national tragedy.

Typically, Soviet policies were copied most slavishly in **Bulgaria,** although the veteran Bulgarian leader Todor Zhivkov was at pains to refute this assessment and claimed that Bulgaria's own *preustroistvo* ("restructuring"—akin to Soviet *perestroika*) had been worked out on the basis only of what was relevant to his country's development. Nevertheless he conceded that *preustroistvo* would have been unthinkable without the Soviet initiatives.

By the beginning of 1988, however, there were indications that over-eagerness by the Bulgarian leadership to emulate Soviet reforms had led to decisions causing widespread confusion. Some observers were prompted to characterize Bulgaria's reforms, which included frequent government reorganizations, radical redrawing of internal regional boundaries, and an initiative completely to dismantle state control of the economy, as "all bustle but no substance". Allegedly this over-eagerness also prompted a caution from the Soviets, with the result that at a special conference of the ruling Bulgarian Communist Party in January 1988 the authorities seemed intent on slowing down the pace of *preustroistvo* and on dampening expectations of rapid political, economic and social transformations.

Moreover, the sincerity of the Bulgarian leadership's commitment to reform was called into question by the sacking of two of its most prominent reformers in July 1988, although it was unclear whether this represented a conservative backlash or the consequence of a failed "palace coup" against Zhivkov.

Czechoslovakia adopted in 1987 a programme of economic "restructuring" (*prestavba*) nominally inspired by Soviet *perestroika,* but this did nothing to change the common Western assessment that the Czechoslovak leadership would not seek to emulate the far more general and radical Soviet reforms. It appeared that the Czechoslovak leadership could not attempt any major departure from its policies of the past two decades without calling into question the legitimacy of the "normalization" programme adopted following the removal in 1968–69 of the reformist administration at the time of the "Prague Spring", led by Alexander Dubcek. Indeed, in official statements in 1987 and 1988 the leadership was at pains to refute suggestions that *prestavba* could be likened to the liberalization under the Dubcek administration.

Although some Czechoslovak leaders tried to promote an image of harmony with Soviet policy, official discussions during a visit by Gorbachev in April 1987 were described as "frank", a euphemism commonly denoting differences of opinion. Nevertheless, in his major speech of the visit Gorbachev stated that "we are far from appealing to every socialist country to copy us", but stressed the need for "obligatory respect" by each of the countries of Eastern Europe for the interests of its allies.

The enduring hardline positions of Czechoslovakia's leaders were demonstrated most graphically in the harsh treatment of dissidents who, inspired in part by the liberalizing trends in the Soviet Union, took to the streets of the Czechoslovak capital, Prague, with increasing frequency. In early 1987 this prompted one senior Czechoslovak Communist Party figure to condemn people who "sponge on the changes in the Soviet Union while hiding their anti-social and anti-socialist activity".

A clear indication of reservations in **East Germany** towards Soviet reform policies was given in April 1987 by the East German leader Erich Honecker when he stated that democratic and open discussion was already a reality in East German political life, and claimed that thanks to reforms implemented since 1971 the country already had "an efficient and functioning system of economic and social planning". Shortly beforehand another prominent member of the East German leadership had stated categorically that East Germany was not obliged to follow the Soviet lead in reforms.

The East Germans were particularly critical of Soviet *glasnost* and the reappraisal of Soviet history. The authorities frequently prevented the appearance of controversial Soviet press reports in East Germany, and in mid-1988 they went so far as to ban distribution of a liberal Soviet magazine.

The East European ally most out of step with the Soviet reforms was **Romania,** where the increasing despotism of President Nicolae Ceausescu and his almost Stalinist policies brought widespread international condemnation and put severe strain on relations with the Soviet Union. When Gorbachev visited Romania in May 1987 many of his public statements, including criticisms of the lack of Romanian *glasnost,* were ignored by the Romanian media, and the strictly regimented audience at a public rally gave him an unenthusiastic reception. By contrast, there were wild ovations for Ceausescu's speech, in which he announced pointedly that co-operation and the forces of socialism would increase only "by respecting the right of each country to decide its own development, path and forms". The Romanian leadership insisted that it had been implementing reforms akin to *perestroika* since Ceausescu's coming to power in 1965.

For Ceausescu's return visit to the Soviet Union in October 1988, Gorbachev appeared to deliver a deliberate snub by failing to appear at the official airport welcoming ceremony, and at a lunch in Ceausescu's honour Gorbachev's speech included several scarcely veiled criticisms of Romania's resistance to reform and its poor human rights record. Furthermore, a leading dissident member of the Romanian Communist Party was given a warm high-level welcome when he visited Moscow in December 1988, and there were even suggestions that the Soviet authorities might have given their blessing to an attack on Ceausescu in an open letter issued in March 1989 by six former members of the Romanian leadership, possibly in the hope of fomenting an anti-Ceausescu mutiny.

The less authoritarian and interventionist Soviet approach towards the allies in Eastern Europe meant that not only were their disagreements with the Soviet Union allowed into the open, but that so too, inevitably, were their differences with each other. The most vociferous exchanges developed between Romania and Hungary, with Hungary trying to draw international attention to the plight of Romania's Hungarian minority, but there were numerous lesser arguments, especially over visa requirements and trade tariffs. Many of the latter were conducted in the forum of the Council for Mutual Economic Assistance (Comecon—the socialist trading bloc grouping together the Soviet allies in Eastern Europe, and Cuba, Mongolia and Vietnam). By 1989 this body appeared to be struggling to overcome stagnation in its members' reciprocal trade relations and deep divisions between the reformist and conservative member states, and was even threatened with the prospect of its most reformist member, Hungary, breaking ranks altogether and reorienting itself, at least in economic terms, decisively towards the West.

FOREIGN AFFAIRS: THE "GLOBAL DIPLOMATIC OFFENSIVE"

In line with the reforms in the economic, social and cultural spheres, and the explicit rejection of the practices of the 1970s, observers also began to talk of a "global diplomatic offensive" intended to revive a foreign policy which, it was generally agreed, had been largely moribund since the mid-1970s. The way in which Soviet foreign policy was conducted changed radically almost as soon as Gorbachev took power, and particularly following Gromyko's replacement as Foreign Minister by Shevardnadze.

The most notable new feature of relations with Western countries was that the Soviet Union increasingly assumed the initiative in disarmament negotiations with the United States, and mounted a skilful propaganda campaign which appeared to take the US administration by surprise, and at times had it on the defensive. The improvements in Soviet human rights observance were also regarded as evidence of a desire to defuse an issue which had previously hindered diplomatic contacts with the West and had disrupted trade relations. Moreover, in all of Gorbachev's and Shevardnadze's foreign visits, observers noted what became known as the "charm offensive", with the new Soviet leader and his Foreign Minister, usually accompanied by their fashionable wives, presenting to the world a much more amiable face than their dour predecessors.

The first example of the new Soviet offensive on disarmament came just a month after Gorbachev took office as CPSU leader, when he declared a moratorium on the deployment of Soviet medium-range missiles in Europe; in July 1985, Gorbachev announced a unilateral moratorium on nuclear weapons testing. During a visit to France in October, his first to the West as Soviet leader, he proposed a 50 per cent reduction in long-range nuclear missiles in conjunction with a complete ban on space-based weapon systems (an allusion to the US SDI or "star wars" programme), and separate negotiations on nuclear arms reductions with France and the United Kingdom.

An invitation to a summit meeting with US President Ronald Reagan had been delivered immediately after Gorbachev's election as CPSU general secretary, while US foreign policy reviews began to suggest a more flexible and less confrontational US attitude towards the Soviet Union, even though both sides continued to take a hard line in official pronouncements. The summit (the first between Soviet and US leaders since Brezhnev had met Jimmy Carter in Vienna in 1979 to sign the SALT II Treaty) took place in Geneva in November 1985. While a series of meetings between Gorbachev and Reagan produced no tangible results, it was generally deemed a success because of the apparent development of a personal rapport between the two men.

Gorbachev and Reagan met again in October 1986 at Reykjavik in Iceland, for what was variously described as a "mini-summit" or a "pre-summit". The two-day meeting had been announced less than two weeks before, the entirely unexpected announcement coming at the end of a month of controversy and strain in Soviet–US relations over the so-called "Daniloff affair", involving the arrest and month-long detention in Moscow of the US journalist Nicholas Daniloff, apparently in retaliation for the arrest for spying of a US diplomat in New York.

The Reykjavik discussions went on for far longer than scheduled, giving rise to intensive speculation and growing excitement that a dramatic agreement on disarmament might be in the offing. There was a corresponding sense of disappointment when it was finally announced that no agreements had been concluded on intermediate nuclear forces, strategic weapons reductions or other issues, apparently because of Soviet insistence on an overall package, to include SDI. Reagan had reportedly been carried along almost to the point of accepting this package, but ultimately had been unwilling to make sufficient concessions on SDI to satisfy Soviet demands. Following the summit, Gorbachev attributed to the US negotiators the responsibility for failing to respond to Soviet initiatives and concessions, and he appeared to win world opinion to his side.

The inconclusive Reykjavik discussions at first appeared to complicate and further strain relations between the two countries. However, at the beginning of 1987, both sides signalled their willingness to separate the issue of intermediate nuclear forces (INF) from the more complex and contentious problem of strategic arms. Discussion moved forward in the course of the year to the announcement in September of an agreement in principal on INF.

The Treaty on Intermediate Nuclear Forces, providing for the elimination over a three-year period of all intermediate-range land-based nuclear weapons held by the Soviet Union and the United States, was initialled during a Reagan-Gorbachev summit meeting in Washington in December 1987. Although the treaty affected less than 7 per cent of the nuclear warheads owned by the two superpowers, it was the first ever agreement to eliminate a whole category of offensive nuclear weapons, and was regarded by both sides as a prelude to further agreements covering strategic nuclear weapons and other aspects of the military balance. The agreement also involved the mutual acceptance of an unprecedentedly intrusive regime of inspection of each other's weapons facilities to verify compliance with the treaty, as well as the acceptance by the Soviet Union of the principle of asymmetry in arms reductions, by which it would be required to eliminate twice as many missiles as the USA.

Reagan visited Moscow at the end of May 1988 for a summit which featured the formal signing of the INF treaty following its ratification by the Senate and the Supreme Soviet. In statements following the talks, both leaders spoke of their satisfaction with the improvements in Soviet–US relations, with Reagan commenting: "Quite possibly we are beginning to break down the barriers of the post-war era".

The Soviet withdrawal from Afghanistan, reductions in the military presence in the Soviet Far East and Mongolia, and pressure on Vietnam to withdraw its troops from Cambodia, were the key elements in efforts to improve Soviet standing in Asia, notably its relations with China and Japan.

The military involvement in Afghanistan since the end of 1979 was considered a major hindrance to Soviet foreign policy in Asia. Within a year of taking office as CPSU leader, Gorbachev had heralded a change in the official attitude when he called the war there a "bleeding wound", and gradually it came to be regarded publicly in the Soviet Union as yet another policy disaster of Brezhnev's last years. The war was unpopular with the public, was a huge drain on military and other resources, and ultimately cost the lives of some 15,000 Soviet troops.

In his first announcement of a major foreign policy initiative towards Asia, Gorbachev announced in a speech in the far eastern city of Vladivostok in July 1986 that six Soviet regiments were being withdrawn from Afghanistan. This was intended to give further impetus to a political settlement of the conflict there. By this time the question of a timetable for a complete Soviet troop withdrawal was the only unresolved issue in a four-part UN peace plan, but in February 1988 Gorbachev suddenly announced major concessions on this issue. Two months later an agreement signed by the Soviet Union, Afghanistan,

Pakistan and the United States for a Soviet withdrawal within nine months was put into effect. The last Soviet soldiers left Afghan soil in mid-February 1989.

Gorbachev's Vladivostok speech also featured the announcement that the withdrawal of "a substantial portion" of Soviet troops from Mongolia was "under review", and that the Soviet Union was willing to discuss the reduction of land forces elsewhere in the vicinity of the border with China, as well as the disputed demarcation of that border. Gorbachev also stated that the Soviet Union was prepared "at any time and at any level to discuss with China questions of additional measures for creating a good-neighbourly atmosphere".

Sino-Soviet normalization talks, which had been taking place since 1982, were given considerable impetus by this new Soviet willingness to discuss the most contentious issues, and by a partial withdrawal of Soviet troops from Mongolia in mid-1987. Over the next two years, relations improved considerably. Shevardnadze visited China in February 1989, and in official talks it was agreed that Gorbachev should go to the Chinese capital, Beijing, in May for the first summit with Chinese leaders since 1959. Furthermore, it was announced in March 1989 that 75 per cent of Soviet troops in Mongolia were to be withdrawn.

In the past, China had insisted upon a settlement of the issue of Cambodia (where the Soviet Union supported the Vietnamese-backed government but China supported the tripartite coalition government-in-exile) as a necessary precursor to high level talks with the Soviets. During Shevardnadze's February 1989 visit, a joint statement was drawn up on Cambodia outlining the main issues of agreement and disagreement. The steady improvements in Sino-Soviet relations had already contributed to enhanced diplomatic efforts towards a settlement in Cambodia, including a timetable for a Vietnamese troop withdrawal.

Relations with Japan also benefited from the Soviet willingness to reduce its military presence in Asia, and as early as the beginning of 1986 Moscow had signalled its intention to improve diplomatic contacts when Shevardnadze visited Japan, marking a resumption of high-level meetings after a lapse of nearly 10 years. However, the new Soviet leadership made little progress in resolving the main issue hindering a major improvement in Japanese-Soviet relations, namely Japanese insistence that the Soviet Union negotiate on the status of a group of formerly Japanese islands which the Soviet Union had annexed in 1945.

Elsewhere in the world, the Soviet Union set about imparting new vigour to its contacts with developing countries, no longer confining itself to exchanges with its established allies but even entering into dialogue with sworn ideological foes, such as South Africa. Improvements in relations with the developing world undoubtedly benefited from the moves towards settlement of regional conflicts involving Soviet or Soviet-backed forces, notably Afghanistan, Cambodia and Angola, as well as from Moscow's willingness to offer itself as mediator in disputes between states, and from the renunciation of doctrines endorsing Soviet military adventures in other countries and the export of Marxist-Leninist revolution.

Gorbachev's influence went as far in reshaping the conduct of foreign policy as in any other area of Soviet life, and his first four years in office were marked by more realism and pragmatism than at probably any time in the history of Soviet diplomacy.

Breakdown in Red Square (*Liba Taylor/Select*)

Softer drinks for harder times? (*Liba Taylor/Select*)

PART II

REPORTAGE
EXPERT BRIEFINGS
REFERENCE SECTION

REPORTAGE
DREAMS OF FREEDOM AT CAFÉ MOSCOW
Tim Whewell

In shop windows in the main street of Vilnius, the capital of Soviet Lithuania, you can see a poster depicting a large old fashioned mincing machine. On one side, ribbons in the national colours of the three formerly independent Baltic republics disappear between the blades. What comes out on the other side is, not surprisingly, red. It's the kind of illustration that even a year ago, could have earned a long gaol sentence for anti-Soviet activity. Today, the only passers-by who appear startled are foreigners.

First to change have been names: Soviet Square in the centre of Vilnius will be retitled Rebirth Square. Lenin Avenue is out; Gediminas Avenue—named after the medieval Grand Duke of Lithuania—is coming in. Anything that relates to the past seems to be good—particularly, anything dating back to the Baltic Republics' brief 20 years of independence before 1940.

In the Lithuanian capital, trumpeters in pre-war officers' uniforms of bottle green with golden braid herald the speakers, at a meeting called by *Sajudis*—the grass-roots reform movement. Speakers include an 11-year-old representative of the Republic's Scouting movement—banned for 40 years and now revived. Nostalgia in the neighbouring republic of Latvia has a more down-to-earth object. In the capital, Riga, I found a long line of citizens queuing for two hours to see a recently-opened exhibition dealing with Latvia's achievements between the wars. Inside, the biggest crowds were gathered round a display with models of light sports planes and Minox cameras—the kind of high technology goods that Latvia used to export to Western Europe before the war, and which it no longer manufactures.

But perhaps the best illustration of what the Balts feel they have lost over the last 50 years comes from Estonia. In one of the main squares of the capital, Tallinn, stands the Café Moscow. It's a rather gloomy place with plain wood-panelled walls, surly waitresses, and little on the menu except instant coffee, two kinds of cakes, or boiled fish and rice. Every few weeks, however, an old man of about 80 totters into the café—and receives more attention than any ordinary customer could expect. His name is Nikolai Kultas—and he's become a national celebrity in Estonia since he appeared on local TV recently to tell the story of the café. . . For he was the man who founded it back in 1936, and who ran it for four years until the Soviet occupation. Then, the café was nationalized and Mr Kultas was sent to a Russian prison camp. Before that, he says, the café offered 12 kinds of

coffee and 72 varieties of cake. The waitresses were multilingual, there were
newspapers from all over Europe, and if you came in off the night train with
a crumpled suit, a boy would take it away and press it while you sat and had
your breakfast.

Estonians are entranced by such details of the past. They believe that,
given independence, they would in time live no worse than the Finns, the
Danes, or the Dutch. But the non-Estonian immigrants to the republic, who
now make up nearly half the population, believe such ideas are dangerous
fantasy. At a meeting of their organization, the Interfront, in a factory club
in the grim industrial suburbs of Tallinn, speakers insisted that it was they,
the immigrants, who were responsible for turning backward Estonia into a
developed country after the war. An old war veteran—his jacket covered
with medals—rose to denounce the new law which makes Estonian the
official language of the republic. To massive applause, he declared the
law would reduce him and his children to the status of *gastarbeiters* or
second-class citizens. Afterwards, a group of Russian women gathered round
me, desperately seeking an outsider who might prove sympathetic. With tears
in their eyes, they insisted they wanted to learn Estonian, but there were no
classes, no books, no lessons on TV or radio. . . The native population, they
said, didn't really want them to learn the local language, it just wanted them
to leave.

Most of the Russian immigrants at that meeting lived in the huge
estates of high-rise flats that ring Tallinn, identical to ones you can
find in any city in the Soviet Union. Native Estonians shudder at the
very mention of those estates, preferring to live in small detached private
houses which they often build themselves. In Estonia, and elsewhere in the
Baltic, therefore, a physical separation of the population along ethnic lines
often emphasizes the division in attitudes. Trying to bridge this division are
the local Communist Party bosses. Mostly appointed last year, their informal
manner and even their comparatively youthful physical appearance marks them
out as quite different to party leaders elsewhere in the USSR. Mikk Titma,
for example, the Estonian ideology secretary, discards the usual collar and tie
when making televised policy statements. He prefers polo-necked sweaters.
Meanwhile, in Latvia, I found the Communist chairman of the Supreme
Soviet, Anatoly Gorbunov, sitting unannounced among other delegates at
a conference of the grass-roots Popular Front movement. He rose from
his seat—almost bashfully—only when a speaker on the platform called
on him—by first name—to share his impressions of a recent meeting with
Mikhail Gorbachev.

AT HOME ON REVOLUTION DAY

Helen Womack

Gleb Franzovich Weiss, a 32-year-old joiner from Leningrad, has finally managed to beat the housing crisis and moved out of his parents' home. He has left the large room with puce striped wallpaper and high ceiling where Franz Richardovich, his ethnic German father, and Galina Pavlovna, his Siberian-born mother, sleep, eat and watch television, and moved one door down the corridor of the communal flat housing four families to the little blue room occupied by a neighbour until he died not long ago. Now, if he wished, Gleb could bring a girl back to share the single bed in the corner of his room. So far, he has limited himself to getting the dog he always wanted, a poodle he has called *Bely* (Snowie) in a play on his own surname.

Gleb's room is sparsely furnished. A photo enlarger which looks as if it belongs in a museum is piled with other junk on top of a wardrobe. Apart from this, there is an armchair and a table covered with literary journals such as *Novy Mir*. Gleb is reading Anatoly Rybakov's *Children of the Arbat*, a long-suppressed exposé of the Stalin era. He is typical of the majority of Soviet citizens, who have benefited enormously from the greater intellectual freedom of *glasnost,* but whose material standard of living, despite *perestroika,* has improved hardly at all.

Because of waiting lists of 10 years and more for self-contained state flats in the high-rise suburbs, it will be a long time before Gleb can hope for anything better than the "communalka". The government has promised that every family will have its own flat by the year 2000 but millions of Soviet people still live communally. The former capital, built by Peter the Great using European engineers including perhaps Gleb's ancestors, has more communal flats in rambling old buildings than many more modern Soviet cities, although the local authorities are gradually moving people out in order to renovate the housing stock.

To a Western visitor, the communal flat can seem romantic. Gleb's is just off the main Nevsky Prospekt on a fine boulevard of 19th century apartments with wrought iron balconies looking down on to a row of plane trees. Neighbours are always dropping in on each other and everyone knows the others' business. With people living so close together, it would be impossible for an old person to die and lie unnoticed for weeks until the smell or mounting milk bottles alerted strangers. But the claustrophobia and lack of privacy can be hard to endure. Gleb points to the stairwell where one woman from the flat threw herself to her death in a moment of despair. Another neighbour hanged herself in her room some years ago.

While being forced to share, the residents try to maintain their separate dignities and there is a strong sense of property. In the narrow bathroom which serves nine people, there are four shelves. The Weiss family keep their soap on the top shelf and warn visiting guests against using the neighbours' toiletries by mistake. Likewise, it is important to know the demarcations of the kitchen, with its four stoves and four crockery cupboards. In the *communalka,* you are welcome to borrow but you must not help yourself without permission.

The system is carried to absurdity in the tiny toilet where four light bulbs are connected to four switches leading to four separate electricity meters. The pile of paper strips torn from *Leningradskaya Pravda* seems, however, to be for common use. Of course, there is always a queue for the loo. As you approach it, you see Mr Vasilyev in his vest and braces furtively open the door of his room, swear quietly to himself that you have beaten him to it and close the door again.

The flat-dwellers show consideration for each other by discouraging friends from telephoning after 11 p.m. and by generally trying to avoid noise. But inevitably, in this microcosm of Soviet society, somebody is having a birthday party when somebody else has a headache. The best time for a drunken binge therefore is a public holiday.

On November 7, the guests always arrive early at Galina Pavlovna's to watch the Leningrad Revolution Day demonstration pass the Hermitage on local television. There is a great commotion at the door as muddy boots are exchanged for slippers and coats are taken and laid in the curtained-off cubicle where Gleb's parents sleep.

Despite Mr Gorbachev's anti-alcohol drive, there is vodka on the table and the men are already sampling it by mid-morning while the women are still drinking tea. Galina Pavlovna makes cabbage pasties and the *pelmeni* (meat dumplings) for which she is famous throughout the neighbourhood. Franz Richardovich may get out the family photo album (full of fair-haired characters with Russified German names) or show a crackly home movie of his canoeing holiday in Siberia in 1976.

By afternoon, the women have started drinking too and soon everyone is voluble. Gleb begins to recount some of the gruesome things he has learnt about Stalin through his reading. He should have known better. The merry mood abruptly changes and he finds himself in a row he has had at least 100 times, a row which is widening the generation gap in millions of families across the Soviet Union.

"You cannot blame Stalin," cries Galina Pavlovna at the top of her voice.

"He knew nothing of the killings, it was the evil people all around him." She is nearly 60, a life-long member of the Communist Party. She has a heart of gold but she is too old to discard the beliefs of a lifetime.

Franz Richardovich steps in to restore order. "I will not have a word against Stalin said in this house," he declares, banging his fist on the table. His attitude is all the more difficult for his son to understand because he comes from a people who suffered particularly under Stalin, being deported en masse to Siberia lest they collaborated with the invading Germans.

Gleb gets up and walks out to the streets, which are like a home to him. There he merges with the thousands strolling along the banks of the Neva in honour of the festival, or perhaps escaping from their own domestic tensions.

1. THE POLITICAL FUTURE
Sir Bryan Cartledge

> "Political reform is a kind of oxygen necessary
> for the vital activity of the public organism."
> (*Gorbachev, 29 November 1988*)

THE OBJECTIVE

Gorbachev's critics accuse him of trying to do too many things at once. As if the gargantuan task of restructuring the entire Soviet economy, curing chronic food shortages and raising the quality of Soviet daily life were not enough, he is trying to reform the Soviet political system as well. Even among the supporters of *perestroika*, there are those who argue that by broadening the agenda of reform to an unmanageable extent, Gorbachev is jeopardizing the success of its crucial element, the rescue and resuscitation of the Soviet economy. In a one-party state, moreover, political reform is inevitably the most sensitive dimension of change. It concerns position, privilege and power; and it touches upon the central issue of the authority of the Party itself.

Gorbachev's reply to criticism on these lines is to restate his conviction that every element of his reform programme is interrelated and interdependent. In June 1988 he urged the 19th Party Conference to "have the courage to admit that if the political system remains immobile and unchanged, we will not cope with the tasks of *perestroika*". Gorbachev argued, rightly, that the existing political structure had been proved to be vulnerable to the establishment of unfettered dictatorship, with all the ensuing horrors of Stalinist rule: equally, it encouraged inertia and made possible the degenerative stagnation of the Brezhnev years. A system in which the organs of both the Party and the government hierarchies—the Party Committees and the Soviets respectively—serve simply as transmission centres for directives from above is at the mercy of whoever seizes the levers of power. Gorbachev is very well aware of the limitations and vulnerability of the traditional Russian "revolution from above" which can be, and has been, unmade even more easily than it was made. He is therefore concerned to involve the Soviet people as a whole in political activity, both through direct participation and through the electoral process, in order to make his reform programme less vulnerable to summary reversal. In the belief, probably justified on the whole, that most Soviet people would like his reforms to succeed, Gorbachev is trying to complement and to buttress revolution from above with a measure of revolution from below. Opening the Supreme Soviet's session on constitutional reform in November, 1988, Gorbachev referred to "a question one often hears", namely:

> "Isn't it too early for us to buckle down to political reform without first building a material base for it and achieving a breakthrough in meeting the vital needs of people for food, consumer goods, services and housing? No, comrades, there are no easy ways . . . . . it is only by combining economic reform with political changes, democratization and *glasnost* that we can fulfil both the immediate and the long-term tasks we have set ourselves."

If an economic reform programme which places a premium on decentralization and local initiative is to succeed, Gorbachev must bridge the divide which, both in pre-revolutionary Russia and since the pall of Stalinism descended over the Soviet Union, has separated "us", the ruled, from "them", the rulers. He has to break down the deep scepticism of the whole political process which six decades of single-candidate or single-list "elections" have engendered. When he or she votes, a Soviet citizen has until now been carrying out a civic duty, or more accurately obeying an order, rather than making a choice. The new Soviet Constitution will enable the voter, mostly but not invariably, to make a choice between two or more candidates for membership of any Soviet, from the new Congress of Peoples' Deputies downwards; and the revised Party Statutes will create the same possibility of choice in elections to Party offices.

A Soviet citizen who has been involved both in the selection and election of a political candidate will, for the first time, experience a degree of responsibility for the decisions in which the elected Deputy may be concerned. An element, albeit slender and fragile, of accountability is being introduced into Soviet politics. If it survives and takes root, this could initiate an important psychological change in Soviet society which would affect factory and farm as well as election meeting and voting booth. This, at any rate, is Gorbachev's hope. This is the logic of his definition of *perestroika* as "democratization plus radical economic reform".

In addition to these overt, declared objectives in initiating a programme of political reform, Gorbachev has another purpose which must, of its nature, remain undeclared. It is to accelerate the removal from office of those who, in both the Party and government machines, are actively resisting *perestroika* or quietly suffocating it through procrastination. The most formidable block of opposition to, or at least lack of enthusiasm for, the changes which Gorbachev and his allies are attempting to introduce lies in the Central Committee of the CPSU: the most common estimate is that about one third of its membership, whether from genuine ideological conviction or from selfish career motives, would like to see *perestroika* run into the sand.

The Central Committee is elected by the Party Congress, which is convened only once in five years: the next Congress is due to meet in 1991 and Gorbachev must, therefore, wait until then to attempt to bring about the major changes in the Central Committee's composition which he would certainly like to see. Thanks to the interlocking nature of the Soviet political system, however, he can make useful progress in the interim by enlisting the aid of the Soviet public in removing opponents or doubters from the elected positions—such as that of Mayor of a major city—which in turn entitle them to Central Committee membership. They would still remain members of the Central Committee until 1991, but would not qualify for re-election by the next Party Congress at that time.

Meanwhile, the election of active supporters of *perestroika* to key positions in local government and to membership of the Congress of Peoples' Deputies is, from Gorbachev's point of view, highly desirable for its own sake: that Congress will, after all, elect not only the new-style Supreme Soviet but also its Chairman—the Soviet President—a post which Gorbachev wishes to be sure of retaining. It is already clear that the first round of elections under the new rules have not proved to be a walk-over for the reformists: entrenched political interests in city, town and countryside have been tenacious in defending themselves and adept in squeezing out inconveniently radical spirits. Andrei Sakharov's initial rejection by his own Academy of Sciences as a candidate for the People's Congress is a case in point. But a start has been made; and the new electoral process, a centrepiece of Gorbachev's political reform, seems likely to go some way towards meeting his objective of reinvigorating the organs of Party and Government alike with an injection of new blood.

THE REFORM

The old-style Supreme Soviet, the Soviet Union's former "parliament", was not taken seriously and did not deserve to be. It met, on average, four times a year for one or two days at a time to listen in respectful silence to several hours of speeches by the leadership on the Plan, the State Budget and other matters requiring legislative approval. Until the last months of its life, when some courageous deputies from Estonia dared to abstain and even vote against some provisions of the new Constitution, all motions were passed unanimously, a forest of right arms being raised on command in a depressing ritual.

The new Supreme Soviet, which will have its first session in 1989, is to be very different. With about 540 members, it will be just over a third of the size of its predecessor. More importantly, it will be in session for approximately eight months of the year, instead of eight days. Inevitably, its political complexion will be orthodox: elected by the 2,250 members of the Congress of Peoples' Deputies from amongst their own number (which includes 750 deputies selected by the Party and other "social organizations" rather than elected by the voters), it will contain a high percentage of Party and government worthies and very few, if any, more radical spirits. But deliberative and legislative assemblies of that size tend to generate their own chemistry. The 19th Party Conference, an even less heterogeneous assemblage, showed that 60 years of repression have not deprived Soviet people of their political tongues: it was characterized at times by sharp, hard hitting debate which, filmed for television and reported in the press, in itself contributed to the political education of the Soviet public.

Once the new Supreme Soviet has settled down and become fully conscious of the powers which the new Constitution gives to it, it is likely to do much more than simply rubber-stamp the policies and applaud the speeches of the leadership. Against the background of multi-candidate elections, Supreme Soviet deputies will feel a greater obligation than in the past to be seen to represent the special interests and concerns of their constituencies—economic, environmental and, above all, national. An Armenian deputy who fails to speak up for Armenia, or an Estonian who is weak in the defence of Estonian interests can expect short shrift from his local electorate at the next elections. To an increasing extent, as it finds its political feet, the new Supreme Soviet will become an assembly more deserving of the description "parliament". It will become more aware of its powers and privileges. It will, perforce, develop a more sophisticated committee system to cope with the increased volume of its business. Its proceedings will play an important role in the political education of the Soviet people: they will provide an example to lesser Soviets throughout the Union.

The hierarchy of lesser Soviets, the "parliaments" of the individual republics and the city, town and village councils must be the focus of any political reform which is to stand a chance of enduring. Under Stalin and his successors, the revolutionary slogan of 1917, "all power to the Soviets", had been quickly converted into the reality of "all power to the CPSU". Local Soviets, like the Supreme Soviet itself, became and remained for six decades mere rubber stamps for Party decisions: close interlocking between the Executive Committees of the Soviets and the local Committees of the Party ensured that real power was concentrated in the latter. Over the years, the Party gathered to itself day-to-day control of every aspect of Soviet life, spawning a network of committees and a vast Party bureaucracy in the process. In every community, the Party building was where the power lay: the Soviets, though sometimes more prestigiously housed, became a meaningless facade of bogus "democracy". A central objective of Gorbachev's political reform is to correct this situation. He hopes to re-involve the elected representatives of the people in the daily management of their affairs.

In order to broaden the area of political activity and involvement, Gorbachev must take a measure of power away from the Party, reversing the process of the past 60 years. He aims to restore its original "leading, guiding role", handing over to the Soviets responsibility for local economic management, environmental control and other aspects of local administration. This means that a great many Party officials will lose their jobs—and the privileges which go with them. Gorbachev has already cut the bureaucracy of the Central Committee in Moscow by a swinging 40 per cent. A high proportion of redundant Party officials will simply cross the street to swell the executive staff of their local Soviets, whose new responsibilities will necessitate some reinforcement in expertise; but even if the net reduction in bureaucrats is not as great as Gorbachev would like, they are likely to become—plucked from the impregnable fortress of the Party's authority—more accountable and accessible to the public than hitherto.

It appears, however, that in order to persuade the Central Committee to swallow a contraction of the Party's day-to-day control of Soviet life, Gorbachev was obliged to strike a bargain—indeed, he himself may have flinched from following his policy to its logical conclusion. He told the 19th

Party Conference that "as a rule" First Secretaries of Party Committees, at all levels, should be elected (he actually said in a Freudian slip, "nominated") Chairmen of the corresponding Soviets. If this practice is indeed adopted "as a rule", it could do considerable damage to Gorbachev's political reform: it could make it easy for the Party to retain its grip on every aspect of local affairs and to nip in the bud any tendencies towards "democratization" which might threaten its monopoly of local, as of central, power. Under the beady eye of the local Party First Secretary, ordinary members of Soviets are likely, even in the new political climate, to watch their step and their tongues. Old habits die hard. An optimistic interpretation of the proposal is that it will make Party First Secretaries more accountable to the people at large—if they are not elected to the Chairmanships of their local Soviets the Party, it is hoped, will draw "the appropriate conclusions". We shall see.

This uncomfortable, and potentially dangerous, duality of authority is to be—indeed, already is—reflected at the very top. Gorbachev now combines the post of General Secretary of the Central Committee of the CPSU—leader of the Party—with that of Chairman of the Supreme Soviet—the Head of State. In the latter capacity, he has the power (like the President of the United States) to make nominations to top Government posts, including that of Prime Minister. To quote Gorbachev himself, in his report to the 19th Party Conference:

"Specifically, the President could exercise overall guidance in the drafting of legislation and of major socio-economic programmes, decide on the key issues of foreign policy, defence and national security, chair the Defence Council, submit proposals on nominating the Chairman of the Council of Ministers of the USSR and discharge several other duties traditionally associated with the Presidency."

It is true that Gorbachev's predecessors, from Stalin onwards, exercised the same range of powers *de facto*, simply because the Government and the Soviets were the creatures of the Party. But the new Constitution, designed in theory to "democratize" the Soviet Union partly through a greater separation of powers as between Party and Soviets, in fact formalizes this immense concentration of authority in the hands of one man. Until all other aspects of the political reform have taken firm root, this built-in contradiction could be its Achilles' heel.

THE PROBLEMS

The combination of State leadership with leadership of the Party is not only potentially dangerous but also creates both political and practical problems for the incumbent. If the new Supreme Soviet develops into a genuinely active legislature and authoritative forum for debate, it will require a level of political management by its President going considerably beyond the purely ceremonial appearances which were appropriate to its predecessor. President Gorbachev would be rash to neglect this dimension of his duties and is unlikely to do so. At the same time, however, he must, as General Secretary, manage the Politburo, the Central Committee Secretariat and, through them, the Party. Although in terms of personnel the Supreme Soviet and the Party will overlap to a very considerable extent, the two entities are likely to be jealous of their powers and prerogatives and suspicious of any encroachment upon them.

Circumstances could arise in which Gorbachev might be tempted to use one power base as a lever against the other, for example to mobilize a more radical Supreme Soviet against a more conservative Politburo—or vice versa. Khrushchev, straddling Government (as Prime Minister) and Party (as First Secretary), succumbed to this temptation and was ousted as a result. Particularly with that example before him, Gorbachev will doubtless be more careful. But to ride two horses requires concentration, balance and considerable skill. Given the other distractions inseparable from the position of Head of State—travel abroad, the reception of visiting dignitaries and other forms of ceremonial—Gorbachev faces a Herculean task of political management. He will find it difficult to avoid exposing his back more frequently than political prudence would dictate.

The political reform, however, will encounter deeper problems than those of political management. Perhaps the greatest is the low level of the "political culture" (to use the Sovspeak) of the Soviet people at large. A leading reformist writer, Fyodor Burlatsky, described the problem very well in a recent article (*Literaturnaya Gazeta*, 28 December 1988). He congratulated Gorbachev on his "noble concept" of conducting *perestroika* not only from above, like Khrushchev, but also, through political reform, from below: he pointed out, however, that the process was encountering resistance from the bureaucracy and "the worst representatives of the crowd", who were threatening outright opposition and obstruction. This, said Burlatsky, reflected "the traditions of an authoritarian-patriarchal political culture" and the deformities bequeathed by Stalinism.

Apart from a few chaotic months in 1917, before Lenin unceremoniously dissolved the newly elected Constituent Assembly, the Soviet people have no democratic experience on which to build. This handicap emerged very clearly during the process of selecting candidates, early in 1989, for the new Congress of Peoples' Deputies. Lacking both rules and precedents, the majority of selection meetings were either sterile formalities at which the voters meekly accepted the Party's choice or disorderly shouting matches which, in some cases, had to be closed down without reaching a conclusion. Russian politics, both before and after the Revolution, have been essentially conspiratorial, primarily concerned with seizing power either for or within a party. Every topical issue has been seen in terms of black and white: in the Leninist tradition, there is only one correct answer to any question: wrong answers are not only incorrect but dangerous and must be eliminated. Russians therefore have some experience of destructive polemics but very little of constructive debate. The concept that an opposing view might contain elements of truth which deserve attention is new to them. To quote Burlatsky again: "We need able people who know how to live with an opponent. Certainly not people who . . . crave at least to crush an opponent, to drive him from the platform and, at most, to have him rot in a concentration camp". Gorbachev, too, has shown that he is well aware of the problem: commenting on the political climate at the beginning of 1989, he noted that "everyone is apparently fighting for democracy, while in fact they are calling for strong-arm tactics in dealing with their opponents . . . . Each side sees in the opposing point of view nothing but 'intrigue', unacceptable and inadmissible. How can such discussions be fruitful?"

Gorbachev and his fellow reformers thus have to undertake a massive task of political education. The Soviet people are not yet ready for the climate of greater plurality of opinion without which political reform cannot flourish. The task is not hopeless: the 19th Party Conference showed that, as noted earlier in this chapter. But it will be some time before the Soviet Union's new political institutions settle down to the right balance between excessive docility and obstreperous anarchy.

A further deficiency in Soviet "political culture" derives from the one-party system. Gorbachev has made it abundantly, even brutally, clear that so far as he is concerned the Soviet Union will remain a one-party state: in February 1989 he dismissed any discussion of a multi-party system as nonsense, "foisted on us by irresponsible people, bankrupt of theories and policies, quite bankrupt". Interestingly, he seems unperturbed by the prospect of a multi-party system in neighbouring Hungary; but in the Soviet Union the CPSU's monopoly of power, and even of significant political activity, is to remain unbroken and unchallenged. This has a number of uncomfortable implications and sets obvious limits to Gorbachev's declared objective of "democratization". A specific problem relates to the nature of elections and the quality of political life. In a multi-party system, a candidate represents a group of policies. His (or her) task is to persuade the voters that his party's programme is superior to that of the other parties whose candidates are opposing him. A candidate's personal record and qualities are by no means irrelevant: but they are usually secondary to his or her party's programme in determining which way a vote is cast. In a one-party system, there is only one party programme. There may be differences of emphasis in its presentation as between localities and candidates, but only within a fairly rigid framework of ideology and policy. This means that a candidate's personal qualities become the main criterion by which the voter makes the choice between him and his opponent. Defeat in an election thus amounts to a personal rejection rather than the rejection of an impersonal party programme (unless, as will now be possible but rare in the Soviet Union, a "non-party" candidate defeats a Party candidate at the polls). The possibility of losing what is essentially a local popularity contest is a powerful inhibition against taking part in it: responsible citizens who might otherwise wish to serve their community by playing an active political role are deterred by the implications, both for their careers and for their self-esteem, of defeat. The average calibre of political candidates, and the quality of electoral debate, are lowered. The nation is the loser.

THE UNION

The problems inherent in political dualism, political immaturity and a one-party system, serious though they are likely to prove, are nevertheless dwarfed by that which confronts Gorbachev in the non-Russian republics of the Soviet Union—the "nationalities problem".

The substance of the nationalities problem has been summarized in an earlier chapter. The northern, southern and western peripheries of the Soviet Union consist of non-Russian republics whose territories and peoples have been acquired by Moscow during the past three centuries by military conquest, treaties with defeated opponents and forcible "incorporation". The suppression of the true facts of their histories, the relegation of their languages and cultures to second-class status and the immigration of Russians assured of local preferment have created tensions in the relationship between periphery and centre which Tsarist autocracy and Stalinist dictatorship could repress but not eliminate. With the advent of *glasnost*, these tensions have welled to the surface in one republic after another. At quite an early stage of Gorbachev's

General Secretaryship, people concluded from his open commitment to reform, to the restoration of the rule of law, to decentralization and to "democratization" that the era of naked repression had passed, at least for the time being. They sensed that the risks of voicing their local aspirations, and even of demonstrating for them, had significantly diminished. The demonstrations and riots in Alma Ata, capital of Kazakhstan, against the appointment of a Russian to head the republican Communist Party in December, 1986 showed that they were right.

There is no common pattern to the unrest, and frequently disorder, which occurred during the following two years in several of the non-Russian republics of the Union. The quarrel between Armenia and Azerbaijan over the small "autonomous region" of Nagorny-Karabakh (a predominantly Armenian enclave in Azerbaijan), which has claimed several hundred lives, is not anti-Russian and does not constitute a direct challenge to Moscow's authority. Gorbachev's personal standing has, however, suffered from it. When a delegation of prominent Armenians came to Moscow in February, 1988, to plead for the restoration of Nagorny-Karabakh to their republic Gorbachev should have known better than to encourage them, both by receiving them personally and by promising a "just solution" to the problem. Inevitably, Armenian hopes have been disappointed and Azerbaijanian resentments inflamed. The establishment in Nagorny-Karabakh of a form of direct rule from Moscow is an uncomfortable expedient and unlikely to be permanent. There is simply no way in which both sides can be satisfied. The extent to which the Communist Parties in both republics were side-lined by the disturbances and the fact that the tragedy of the Armenian earthquake appears to have imposed only a temporary truce in the dispute must be deeply worrying to the Soviet leadership.

Moscow is likely to be even more concerned, however, by recent developments in the Baltic republics. The fact that Armenians and Azerbaijanis were able to demonstrate in tens of thousands with relative impunity, evoking nothing more serious than martial law and a curfew from the central authorities, carried its own message to the Estonians, Latvians and Lithuanians during the summer of 1988. They, too, took to the streets and the meeting-halls to commemorate their brief period of independent sovereignty between the two World Wars, to protest against the muffling of their own languages by the Russian tongue and to call for a halt to the tide of Russian immigrants who have been attracted by the higher standard of life on the Baltic seaboard. By contrast with Armenia and Azerbaijan, the Communist Parties in the three republics have by no means been side-lined but, especially in Estonia, have actually taken the lead in voicing national aspirations, including that of independence from Moscow. In Tallinn, the Estonian capital, the Soviet flag has been hauled down, consigned to a museum and replaced by the blue, black and white banner of independent Estonia; the Estonian parliament has resolved that its laws take precedence over the laws of the USSR and appears to be maintaining this position despite being overruled, with contumely, by the Supreme Soviet of the Union. In Latvia and Lithuania, non-Communist "popular fronts", CPSU candidates in the elections to the Congress, of Peoples' Deputies.

Inevitably, developments such as these are contagious. In Georgia, in Byelorussia, in Moldavia, in the Ukraine and even in far-off Yakutia non-Russians are finding their ethnic voices, rediscovering their pasts and calling for a greater degree of local autonomy. In Lithuania, the permitted revival of the Roman Catholic Church has given an additional dimension to national aspiration; in the Ukraine, the proscribed Uniate Church could one day do the same; and in the Moslem republics of Central Asia, Islam is stirring.

To force these diverse and potentially explosive elements back into the rigid Soviet mould from which *glasnost* and the prospect of political reform have released them would be highly dangerous and probably impossible. Gorbachev is in any case well aware of the benefits which could flow from a significant easing of the economic straitjacket which Moscow has up to now imposed on the republics and from allowing them to realize their economic potential as they themselves know best. The Baltic republics in particular, with their more sophisticated infrastructure, more developed work ethic and more recent experience of market economics could serve as a collective showcase for *perestroika* if given their heads. The reform of the Soviet Constitution is already under way. A Central Committee Plenum on the nationalities question is being held in 1989. The mechanisms for change are in place and Gorbachev will doubtless use them. He is likely to share the objectives defined by Burlatsky in the article already cited:

"The general principle is more or less clear: it is necessary to satisfy the legitimate interests of all the nationalities, grant each of them genuine independence and economic and cultural autonomy and, at the same time, recreate a genuine federation and mutually advantageous integration and to strengthen our Union."

Gorbachev himself has pledged (on Feb. 14, 1989) "to try . . . to answer all the questions on the status of the republics, financial autonomy, language, culture and all the rest so that everyone in the country should live well. And unless we solve this, *perestroika* will not happen because the people must feel that with *perestroika* everything changes".

This is by no means a unanimous view. The military, responsible for the defence of Soviet frontiers, will be uneasy over the granting of greater autonomy precisely to those republics on whose territory most of the frontiers lie. The KGB, responsible for internal security, are unlikely to feel comfortable with the greater degree of diversity and national identity which Gorbachev has already permitted. Above all, there are the Russians themselves—living in the most disadvantaged republic of the Union, jealous of the greater economic success and higher living standards achieved by some of the non-Russian republics and opposed to any suggestion of privilege for the "subject peoples" whom they have in the past conquered or absorbed. This adds up to a formidable coalition. Gorbachev is likely to lead the Soviet Union, through the political reform, towards a more genuinely federative structure in which the republics will be freer to order their own economies and domestic affairs: draft amendments to the Constitution have already been prepared with this in view. But he will need all his political skills to achieve this and to navigate the currents of national prejudice, ethnic rivalry and Russian chauvinism which he will encounter.

THE PROSPECTS

Gorbachev clearly faces formidable and daunting problems in carrying forward his political reform, no less than in his attempt to restructure the Soviet economy. He nevertheless has advantages which it would be wrong to underestimate.

The first is the built-in strength of the post of General Secretary of the Party. Four out of the six Commissions into which the apparatus of the Central Committee is now divided are headed by committed Gorbachev supporters. Ligachev and Chebrikov, who head the other two, are not outright opponents of *perestroika* although they clearly have strong reservations about the pace and radical scope of Gorbachev's policies: but they are both too old to pose a serious personal threat to him. In the Politburo, only the Ukrainian boss Scherbitsky (aged 70) and Vorotnikov (62) are survivors from the pre-Gorbachev era: the remainder owe their membership primarily to Gorbachev himself. Gorbachev can therefore rely on the loyalty of most of the key figures in the Party apparatus and in this situation a General Secretary is very hard to dislodge. Lower down the Party hierarchy the picture is less clear-cut. Both in the Central Committee and among the Party rank and file, there are significant pockets of resistance to *perestroika:* but there is, so far, no obvious alternative leader around whom the doubters and resisters might coalesce. Gorbachev has used the powers of his office skilfully to remove or neutralize potential rivals. Given the additional powers of patronage which the Presidency gives him, he is in an extremely strong position. It would take a crisis of exceptional gravity to rupture existing loyalties and change the balance of power in the Central Committee to Gorbachev's disadvantage.

A major crisis can by no means be ruled out. Radical political and economic change is a volatile process. *Perestroika* and *glasnost* have unleashed forces which may prove—indeed, are already proving—difficult to control. It is already clear that if Gorbachev's reforms do take root and produce results, this will only be over a very long timescale—certainly longer than the 10 years for which Gorbachev can hold the office of President after his election by the Congress of Peoples' Deputies. The longer the timescale, the greater the risk that a crisis could arise—in the Baltic republics, in Eastern Europe or elsewhere in the world—sufficiently acute to create a division of opinion in the Politburo and the Central Committee which could change the present pattern and threaten Gorbachev's position.

Gorbachev has had time to show, however, that he is a politician of very considerable skill. Although his instinct, when confronted by an obstacle, is to tread on the accelerator rather than the brake he is capable of tactical retreat when necessary and has proved a good judge of how much the political market will bear at any given moment. Unlike Khrushchev, he will be careful not to allow situations to develop which could create a coalition against him. Like most politicians, he may have to settle for less than he would like to achieve: but he is unlikely to lose his balance.

The subject of this chapter, however, is the political future not of Gorbachev but of the Soviet Union. The one is not necessarily or wholly dependent on the other. The process of political reform which Gorbachev has initiated could be interrupted but it will not, I believe, be reversed. Khruschev put an end to the Stalinist nightmare. The Brezhnev years, the "era of stagnation", were the drugged sleep which often follows nightmares. Now the Soviet people are waking up. *Glasnost* has made them aware, for the first time, of the full horror of Stalinism, of the failures which the Stalinist system bequeathed and, not least, of the abysmal shortcomings of life in the Soviet Union today. Equally, *glasnost* has enabled the Soviet people to compare their lot with that of the peoples of other countries of which they are now allowed to know more. Revelations of the Soviet past have created a new sensitivity to issues of human rights and a new awareness of the importance of the rule of law as an obstacle to tyranny. For these reasons, among others, there is no constituency for a return to the past. The Soviet people sense that there is nowhere to go but forwards. If Gorbachev were to be removed from the scene, the reform process would nevertheless continue, even if less dramatically.

The Soviet people will take time to learn how best to use their new political institutions. The one-party system will preclude the birth of democracy in the Western sense, although there is likely to be a higher threshold of tolerance, within the Party, of diversity of view and of the expression of opinions at variance with the official line. Enough has happened in the Soviet Union since 1985, however, to discredit the belief, not infrequently expressed in the West in the past, that Russians are congenitally incapable of political activity other than blind obedience to the edicts of Tsar or Commissar. Evolution towards a genuinely rational and civilized political society will be slow and, doubtless, occasionally painful. But for the first time in either Russian or Soviet history it has become a realistic prospect.

This optimistic assessment is reinforced by the evidence of the elections to the Congress of Peoples' Deputies which were held on March 26, 1989. These elections were arguably the most important and positive development in the political history of the Soviet Union since 1917—indeed, in many respects they recreated the atmosphere of the heady months between the February and October Revolutions of that year, when the Russian people tested their newly won political freedoms. Not only were prominent radicals such as Boris Yeltsin in Moscow and leading nationalists in the Baltic republics elected to the Congress by massive majorities: but, perhaps even more importantly, the Soviet electorate demonstrated that the exclusion of rival candidates from the ballot papers offered no protection to the Party establishment. In many single-candidate constituencies, the voters simply crossed out the single name offered to them and thus deprived the candidate of the 50 per cent of the vote required for election. Several leading Party figures, including a candidate member of the Politburo and the mayors of Moscow and other major cities, suffered this public humiliation which made their subsequent survival in office improbable. This is exactly the outcome which Gorbachev had been hoping for, although the requirements of intra-Party politics prevented him from acclaiming it too enthusiastically.

The elections also achieved, to a remarkable extent, Gorbachev's other objective—to involve ordinary people in the political process and thereby restore its credibility. The level of popular interest which the elections aroused, shown most dramatically in the demonstrations on the streets of Moscow and other cities in favour of radical candidates, showed that the closed chambers of the one-Party state have been opened to the winds of public approval or disapproval. The new climate will doubtless confront Gorbachev with new problems: there is an obvious danger of backlash from those who have suffered from it and, especially in the non-Russian republics, the more volatile state of Soviet politics will call for skilful management. But Gorbachev embarked on the process of political reform with his eyes open: and although the rapidity with which it is gathering momentum may have surprised him, he is likely to prove capable of riding the waves of change. Presiding over the Soviet Union's political coming-of-age, he is leading his country into a new phase of its history.

2. THE CHALLENGE OF *PERESTROIKA*

David A. Dyker

THE NATURE OF THE PROBLEM

Mr Gorbachev talks openly about the Soviet economy being in a "crisis situation". But how deep is the crisis? One of the areas most affected by *glasnost* is that of official Soviet economic statistics, and a lively debate has developed over the last year or so on the reliability of the official growth indices. In particular, the problem of "concealed inflation" in purportedly constant-price growth indices has been widely aired. At the outset, however, we should emphasize that the essential slowdown in Soviet economic growth rates is as evident from the official statistics of the Brezhnev period as from any other figures. According to contemporary plan fulfilment reports, average growth rates of national income declined from 6 per cent plus for 1965–75 to under 3 per cent by around 1980. CIA[1] recalculations in terms of Western-definition GDP produced exactly the same pattern of slowdown, but suggested that the c.1980 growth rate was in reality no more than 1.0–1.5 per cent. The new conventional wisdom of the *perestroika* period now tells us that growth rates during the "period of stagnation" were in fact near zero.

The clearest statement of the current "official line" comes from a book[2] published in 1988 by Abel Aganbegyan, Gorbachev's senior economic adviser. Aganbegyan argues that an escalating problem of concealed inflation produced a "scissors" movement between reported and real rates of growth in the late

[1]CIA(1988) *Revisiting Soviet Economic Performance under Glasnost: Implications for CIA estimates*, Washington. Dyker, D. A. (1987) "Industrial Planning—forwards or sideways?", in ed. Dyker, *The Soviet Union under Gorbachev: Prospects for Reform*, London, Croom Helm, 1987.

[2]Aganbegyan, A. (1988) *Sovetskaya Ekonomika—vzglyad v Budushchee*, Moscow, Nauka.

Brezhnev period, and claims that in real terms there was virtually no growt
in the Soviet economy during 1981–85. He goes on to assert, however, tha
since 1986 the gap between real and reported growth rates has been largel
closed.

There are two main problems with Aganbegyan's argument. First, can we b
sure that Gorbachev is not simply following the time-honoured Soviet practic
of denigrating previous leaders? The CIA (1988) certainly suspects that ther
is an element of political "rubbishing" in Gorbachev's statistical restructuring
and is sticking to its original estimate of a real rate of growth of around 2 pe
cent for 1981–85. And what of the post-1985 period? Is it really plausible t
suggest that the concealed inflation problem has been solved overnight? Ole
Bogomolov, another trusted Gorbachev adviser, certainly does not think so. I
an article published in early 1989 in the journal *Arqumenty i Fakty* he claime
that the rate of open inflation in the Soviet Union had now reached 5–7 pe
cent. If that is true, and it fits with more impressionistic data, it has certainl
not been accommodated in the "constant price" production series. And wit
growth for 1988 officially reported at 4.4 per cent, simple arithmetic point
directly at the possibility that growth rates in the Soviet Union, even unde
Gorbachev, are actually negative.

But that may not be such bad news as at first it appears. Arguably, the
underlying problem in the Brezhnev period was less one of quantity than o
quality. Attempts to shift the priority from traditionally favoured heavy industry
to consumer goods sectors failed simply because the economy was unable to
generate any impetus at the levels of quality and design required. Attempts to
modernize the Soviet economy through massive transfer of technology from the
West failed because the Soviet economic system was simply not up to the task of
assimilating that technology. Thus the "period of stagnation" was characterized
by lengthening queues, accelerating flight into the secondary economy, and
a growing gap between Soviet and Western technology levels, particularly in
the area of micro-electronics and flexible production systems. If the Soviet
economy is actually contracting right now, in purely physical terms, because
Gorbachev is finally tackling these fundamental structural problems, the price
may be well worth paying. But we must delay judgement on this issue until
we have looked in greater detail at exactly how the restructuring programme
is working out.

INFLATION: PUBLIC ENEMY NO. 1?

Why has the rate of open inflation shot up with *perestroika*? The
lengthening queues of the Brezhnev period reflected the increasing pressure

of repressed inflation, as money wages rose steadily and consumer goods and food production plans remained under-fulfilled. Maintenance of a cheap food policy against the background of stagnating levels of agricultural production intensified the problem and imposed an increasingly onerous burden on the Soviet budget. By the mid-1980s subsidies on meat and dairy products alone accounted for some 10 per cent of Soviet National Income. On the investment side, costs rocketed and returns fell, again imposing a growing burden on the budget which bore little relationship to trends in the production potential of the economy. With total productivity stagnating, or even declining, there was a sense in which the Soviet economy was simply running at a loss in the early 1980s. And as the sources of cheap labour amongst rural and female populations dried up, as sources of cheap energy materials neared exhaustion, so prospects for further economic growth were increasingly pre-empted by those productivity trends. There was, then, little enough to show for the explosion of budgetary expenditure that occurred during the 1970s.

It was part of the mythology of the Brezhnev period that the budget was always balanced. Western specialists suspected different, but it was not until the end of 1988 that Gorbachev's Finance Minister, Boris Gostev, finally gave us a hard figure for the Soviet budget deficit—Rb36.3 billion projected for 1989. By early 1989, however, Bogomolov was telling us that the true figure was around Rb100 billion—some 16 per cent of Soviet national income (the comparable figure for the USA is 3–4 per cent).

The size of the current budget deficit is no doubt partly due to the loss of revenue connected with Gorbachev's anti-vodka drive, and to the collapse in the international price of oil—the Soviet Union's main export—in 1985. Beyond that, it gives us a quantitative indicator of the degree of structural maladjustment in the Soviet economy. Because, furthermore, there is no money market in the Soviet Union, budget deficits can only be financed by printing money. This is essentially where the repressed inflationary pressure comes from. And if effective *perestroika* requires a more flexible, market-oriented system, what is to stop the repressed inflationary pressure turning into a flood of open inflation?

THE IMPORTANCE OF PRICE REFORM

The essential problem for Mr Gorbachev, then, is that *micro-economic* policies, aimed at improving the allocation of resources, may involve all sorts of *macro-economic* complications. Why is price reform so crucial for those micro-economic policies? Essentially because the old system of industrial planning neither required, nor was capable of generating, a set of rational prices. Since enterprises were rewarded for fulfilling output targets rather than responding to market demand, prices played a passive accounting, rather than an active allocative role. Virtually all prices were fixed by the State Prices Committee. With neither the information nor the capacity to calculate scarcity prices, the Committee operated on a crude, cost-plus basis, laced with a good deal of sheer bureaucratic arbitraries. But because enterprises were in any case not at liberty to reallocate resources in response to these changing prices, none of this created any immediate operational problems, at least within industry.

It did, however, create a great many problems in the consumer sector, where buyers were, indeed, free to respond to prices, within the constraint of available supply. It became increasingly clear during the 1980s that food subsidies were not only imposing a massive burden on the budget—they were also inducing appalling wastage of resources. As Gorbachev himself said in his 1987 speech at Murmansk, we have to find a way of stopping children playing football with bread rolls.

Of course, there was also a great deal of waste of resources within industry itself. The tyranny of short-term output targets gave enterprise managers little incentive to economize on materials, and gave them a positive incentive to keep extra workers on their books "just in case". Most importantly, it severely penalized the technologically dynamic manager, since any innovation involving re-tooling is bound to have a deleterious effect on output in the short run. That is why the Soviet leadership now wants to switch the emphasis in the planning system from crude output to profits. But profits are a good indicator only when prices are right. If the prices are wrong, they may be a very bad indicator indeed. There have been cases in recent years where planners have been forced to reimpose compulsory procurement targets for particular crops on farms, simply because the procurement prices for those crops were so out of line with actual scarcities as to produce quite crazy results.

Gorbachev recognizes that it is quite unrealistic, even with modern computer technology, to expect one committee sitting in Moscow to fix every price in the economy. The new principle, then, is that the Prices Committee should set a minimum number of key prices, leaving other prices to be agreed between enterprises. This recognition on the part of the Soviet leadership that good prices mean flexible prices represents a tremendous step forward from the hesitant half-reforms of the past. But it does involve a whole complex of macro-economic complications.

These complications were highlighted towards the end of 1988, as Moscow sought to begin the transition to a system of planning under which central priorities would be safeguarded through a system of "state orders", still essentially imposed by the centre on producing units, leaving the enterprises themselves to sort out other production and delivery schedules on a "direct links" basis. The goal is to transfer the bulk of industrial supply on to decentralized, "wholesale trade" by 1992. But how exactly is the balance of state orders and wholesale trade to be determined? Reports from the beginning of 1988 told us that enterprise capacities were still at that time being loaded up to the hilt with state orders. By September the whole planning system was in turmoil, as managers went into open revolt, threatening to cut deliveries to the state by 15–30 per cent. How would they be able to do this and still fulfil their profit targets? Simple—by raising their prices to other enterprises. It is not difficult to see why open inflationary pressures were building up dramatically at the end of 1988 and the beginning of 1989.

Why is the process of transition so painful? Because the structural imbalances in the Soviet economy are so immense, so deep-seated, that any attempt to resolve them is almost bound to create something akin to chaos in the short run. Here, indeed, is the price the Soviet Union must pay for Brezhnevite stagnation, for the failure, over a period of two decades, to face up to the need for thoroughgoing reform. And it is a price which some Soviet economists would be glad to pay. E. Figurnov, for example, writing in the authoritative *Ekonomicheskaya Gazeta*,[3] argues that as long as there is a massive budget deficit, *perestroika* is bound to bring with it inflation. Any attempt to solve the inflation problem through administrative controls would, however, merely "play into the hands of the opponents of economic reform". The solution, Figurnov argues, is generalized indexation of wages and pensions, as a way of minimizing the social side-effects of an inflation which can only be severe and long-lasting.

SELF-FINANCING AND INCENTIVES

It is not surprising, in the context of the budgetary problem, that Gorbachev has placed primary stress on the need for organizations and individuals to pay their own way. At the enterprise level, the reforms seek to establish the principle of 100 per cent self-financing. The budget should henceforth bear the burden of investment finance only in respect of major new greenfield site projects. All upgrading investment, aimed at modernizing

---

[3]Figurnov, E. (1989) "Tovary—tseny—inflyatsiya", *Ekonomicheskaya Gazeta*, No. 5, p. 14.

existing capacities, should be financed out of enterprise profits, or from bank loans ultimately amortized from enterprise profits. In addition, enterprise management would have increased freedom to use wage and bonus funds as they saw fit, slimming down work forces as appeared necessary and using the savings thus generated to improve incentives for the surviving employees. A wages reform of 1986 sought explicitly to increase industrial differentials, and to ensure that any bonus payments were really earned. While the Soviet government remains committed to full employment, the plans for the period up to the year 2000 imply 13–19 million redundancies. The intention is to absorb these through natural wastage and re-training, and a good deal is being done to develop the system of job placement. But a number of Soviet economists, including liberal gadfly Nikolai Shmelev, argue that the kind of restructuring envisaged is bound to increase the number of unemployed in the Soviet Union. It appears that the jobless total may have increased by around one million in 1988, though that would still leave the country with a rate of unemployment of under 2 per cent.

AGRICULTURE

For most Soviet citizens higher living standards mean in the first instance a better diet. Yet just to maintain present, inadequate levels of food supply, the Soviet Union has to import around 40 billion tonnes of grain per year, imposing a burden of US$5–6 billion on the balance of trade. The output of Soviet agriculture itself has shown no clear upward trend since the early 1970s. The experience of the Brezhnev years, when vast investment expenditures and greatly increased agricultural wages produced virtually no effect, underlined the key importance of the dimension of organizational forms. Locked in the prison-house of Stalin's collective farm, peasants were neither able nor willing to respond to increased resource flows. It was, indeed, Gorbachev himself who was brought to Moscow in 1978 to take over the agriculture portfolio within the Party Secretariat and try to sort out the mess. But for all his previous success as a regional agricultural administrator in Stavropol, for all the manifest good sense of many of his policy initiatives, Gorbachev achieved little during his years as agriculture supremo. It is, perhaps, not surprising, then, to see a progressive radicalization of the Soviet President's approach to this, the most crisis-ridden sector in the Soviet economy. By late 1988 Gorbachev had clearly decided that the future of Soviet agriculture lay in a programme of de facto *privatization*.

In March 1989 Gorbachev announced a series of crucial measures aimed at breaking out of the vicious circle of poor performance and weak motivation once and for all. Having roundly condemned Stalin's collectivization policy, the Soviet leader mapped out a future for Soviet agriculture which would be centrally based on a system of lease-holding (*arenda*). Under this proposal, farmers would rent land from the state on a long-term (c.50-year) basis, and would be free to farm it as they saw fit, subject to the obligation to look after the land properly, and to fulfil contractual commitments freely entered into. A fully-fledged lease-holding system would amount to virtual decollectivization, with the managerial and agronomic staffs of the *kolkhozy* and *sovkhozy* being liquidated. The individuals affected by that liquidation would be free to join the lease-holding collectives, or to offer their services as consultants on a paid basis. To underline his commitment to the principle of returning sovereignty over agriculture operations to the farmers concerned, Gorbachev also proposed abolition of the unwieldy pyramid of agricultural administration headed by Gosagroprom—the State Agro-Industrial Commission. At a meeting with farmers in October 1988 Gorbachev explicitly endorsed the individual family farm as a key element in the Soviet agriculture of the future, and appeared favourably inclined towards the idea that it should be possible for lease-holders to pass on their leases to their children. This is perhaps the most radical idea that *perestroika* has produced to date. But the theme of privatization has not been restricted to agriculture.

CO-OPERATIVES

After the promulgation in 1987 of a disappointing law on private enterprise as such, bearing all the marks of a political compromise, 1988 saw the appearance of a much more important piece of legislation on co-operatives. The new co-operatives would operate on a limited liability basis, and would be allowed to employ outside labour, with wages and working conditions subject to individual contract. Distribution of co-operative income is decided exclusively by the members themselves and co-operatives have complete freedom as regards sales and purchase contracts, though they are subject to elements of central price control. They may raise capital by issuing shares, but only to their own members and employees. In the middle of 1988 co-operatives were employing between 100,000 and 200,000 people, mainly in service sectors. Some Soviet economists have suggested that they could ultimately account for as much as 10–12 per cent of Soviet GNP.

FOREIGN TRADE

It was always a golden rule of the Leninist/Stalinist state that all foreign trade should go through the central state apparatus. Only in this way, the founders of the Soviet Union thought, could a socialist state survive in a capitalist world and stand up to the might of the international companies. But while the foreign trade monopoly has, over the years, certainly enabled the Soviet Union to push the terms of trade in its favour, it has been less efficient at ensuring that the country was importing and exporting the right things, least efficient of all in ensuring that imports of producer goods were utilized efficiently in the domestic economy. The collapse of world oil prices in 1985 suddenly made these problems much more pressing. This, in a nutshell, is why Gorbachev abolished the Ministry of Foreign Trade and the whole system of bureaucratic trade planning centred on it in 1986–87.

Under the new system, as consolidated and extended in a decree of December 1988, all Soviet enterprises are, in principle, now allowed to participate directly in foreign trade, and to retain a proportion of their hard currency earnings for spending on imported materials and equipment, and even imported consumer goods. These measures are clearly aimed at extending the self-financing principle into the foreign trade sphere. Since 1987 foreign ownership of equity in the Soviet Union has been permitted. The maximum foreign share in a joint venture was initially limited to 49 per cent, but was raised to 80 per cent at the end of 1988. Joint ventures are subject both to profits tax (basic rate 30 per cent) and repatriation tax (basic rate 20 per cent), but with a tax "holiday" for foreign partners for two years from the date on which the profits are first generated. They are not subject to the authority of domestic planning bodies, and may be headed by a foreign general director. By the end of 1988 a total of 178 joint venture deals had been signed, mostly with Western partners, though the bulk of them are on fairly small scale. The Soviet authorities are now seeking 'concrete proposals' for a gradual transition to partial ruble convertibility, and have announced plans to set up a Chinese-style Special Economic Zone in the Soviet Far East. The December 1988 decree specifies a number of extra inducements for firms to set up in that region.

CONCLUSIONS

There cannot be the slightest doubt, then, that *perestroika* is for real, that Gorbachev's economic reform programme is the most radical the Soviet Union has seen since the beginning of the First Five-Year Plan. But it is riddled with complications and contradictions. Let us start by going back to the central features of the planning reform itself. The principle of self-financing has, as we saw, generally been taken further than the principle of decentralizing industrial supplies. This immediately raises the problem: how does a successful enterprise, replete with retained profits, go about procuring the machines, bricks etc. to realize its decentralized investment plans? If all its requirements are available on an across-the-counter, wholesale trade basis, then there is no problem. But the reform of the industrial supply system has certainly not reached that stage yet. We can make exactly the same point on the consumption side. What use is it allowing enterprises to pay their workers more money, if there is nothing in the shops for them to spend it on? Gorbachev is perfectly justified in telling the Soviet people that they cannot expect miracles overnight. The Soviet people are equally justified in telling their President that until *perestroika* puts something on the table, it can hardly be expected to produce the kind of motivation revolution which the principle of self-financing aims to foster.

There is exactly the same complex of problems with the foreign trade reform. It is fine saying that joint ventures should not be under the authority of the Plan, but how, in that case, are they to obtain supplies from Soviet enterprises which *are* under the authority of the Plan, and which may have neither the capacity nor the incentive to take on "extra orders"? And how are exporting enterprises, with their foreign exchange accounts, to "translate" dollars into rubles for purposes of calculating wages, bonuses etc? In practice the answer is a bewildering array of coefficients which tends to increase rather than decrease the incidence of bureaucracy.

Of course the Soviet authorities are aware of these problems, and indeed many of the clauses of the December 1988 decree address them. Ruble convertibility will get rid of the coefficients problem. Special Economic Zones will permit the setting-up of whole complexes of enterprises working on a marketized basis, so that joint ventures will be able to obtain supplies from ancillary enterprises which are, like them, free of the tutelage of the plan. In addition, the decree predicates establishment of a system whereby non-exporting enterprises supplying exporting enterprises will receive a definite share of the total final hard currency flow. Thus the purely technical contradictions within the *perestroika* programme are certainly soluble, though only through continuous radicalization of the programme. The political contradictions may be less easily resolved.

In February 1989 Yegor Ligachev told a conference of senior administrators (his speech was televised) that the way to solve the food supply problem is through developing the system of state and collective farms. Talking in terms reminiscent of Brezhnev and Chernenko ("We will drench agriculture with resources"), Ligachev spoke of the need to develop a modern food industry through a centralized programme of investment and restructuring. He did not mention the lease-hold system at all. Significantly he was addressing precisely the people whose jobs are most at risk from Gorbachev's lease-hold proposals.

After the March 1989 Plenum at which Gorbachev reiterated his endorsemen of the lease-hold system, Ligachev went on record with a statement tha there were no agricultural policy disagreements between him and the Sovie President. This is obviously untrue. What does seem to exist is some kind o agreement to differ between the No.1 and the No.2. This may make politica sense, but it is bad news for agriculture. It will replace policy impetus witl policy vacuum in precisely the sector that most desperately needs a completel new approach. It will slow up development of the lease-hold system to ; dangerous extent, and in so doing could jeopardize the momentum of the entire *perestroika* movement.

But when Ligachev tries to stem the tide of radical reform, he speaks no only to the bureaucrats whose jobs are threatened. There are many ordinary people in the Soviet Union who are profoundly anxious about the implication of *perestroika*, with its package of bigger carrots—and bigger sticks—and it promise of price increases on a dramatic scale. Many Soviet people remair deeply attached to the egalitarian principle, deeply suspicious of the profi motive, and only too ready to believe that the only way you can make ; lot of money is by exploiting other people. Nowhere are these attitude more evident than in relation to the co-operatives. While many Sovie citizens have been delighted to be able to obtain better quality services even at higher prices, 1988 witnessed a steady swing in public opinion against the co-operatives. And when the authorities issued a decree ii December 1988 sharply restricting co-operative activity in some areas, they were surely responding to public opinion as well as expressing conservative bureaucratic prejudice. They were also quite simply trying to damp down the fires of inflation. Thus we come back to the technical problems of a radica economic reform which remains crucially incomplete. The great danger fo *perestroika* is that political difficulties may slow down the pace of reform to such an extent that the internal tensions which the reform programme inevitably generates may end up as destructive rather than creative ones.

3. SOVIET FOREIGN POLICY: A NEW REALISM

Stephen Dalziel

The withdrawal of Soviet troops from Afghanistan marked the end of an era in Soviet foreign policy and the beginning of a new period based on Mikhail Gorbachev's much-proclaimed New Political Thinking. As long ago as November 1985, after the "fireside summit" with President Reagan in Geneva, Gorbachev described Afghanistan as "a bleeding wound" for the Soviet Union, and the withdrawal of Soviet forces began to seem a genuine possibility. Gorbachev had already begun to apply his policy of *perestroika* to Soviet foreign policy. In July of that year Andrei Gromyko was "elevated" to the post of state president, after a 30-year spell as Soviet foreign minister. Although Mr Gromyko had undoubtedly served Soviet interests well, he had also created the image of Soviet foreign policy as an inflexible set of rules. This was based on the notion of class struggle and achieving and maintaining the USSR's position as a military superpower. The theory held that all countries, especially developing countries, were heading towards socialism. Mr Gromyko, and the theory, refused to be shaken when reality plainly disagreed with them, most notably with the failure in the 1970s of Soviet policy towards the Middle East.

It is now recognized that this lack of flexibility was a major obstacle to the development of Soviet relations with the rest of the world. Since the Geneva Accords on Afghanistan were signed in April 1988 there has been a far greater willingness to admit the mistakes of the past. Writing in the government newspaper, *Izvestiya*, one of the leading Soviet commentators on foreign policy, Aleksandr Bovin, described both the decision to send troops into Afghanistan and the deployment of SS-20 missiles in Europe as "own goals which led to a decline in our authority on the world stage". Even more significantly, the Soviet foreign minister, Eduard Shevardnadze, criticized the

past conduct of Soviet foreign policy from an ideological standpoint. At the
25th Communist Party Congress in 1976, Leonid Brezhnev said that the era
of detente provided a better foundation for intensifying the class struggle.
Addressing a major conference on Soviet foreign policy and diplomacy in
Moscow in July 1988, Mr Shevardnadze described as deviations from Leninist
policy Khrushchev's famous "We will bury you!" outburst against the capitalist
nations and Brezhnev's attempts to utilize detente for class struggle. He
recognized that these had helped to contribute to an "enemy image" for the
Soviet Union.

But it was not only internationally that the USSR had suffered through
the conduct of its foreign policy. Domestically, too, people had grown cynical.
Whilst this may not have mattered to the Soviet leadership of the 1970s and
early 1980s, in the age of the New Political Thinking the opinion of Soviet man
is held to count. At the 19th Communist Party Conference in Moscow in the
summer of 1988, one speaker, criticizing the decision in 1979 to send troops into
Afghanistan, declared that even candidate members of the Politburo learned
about the intervention from the newspapers. (This was clearly an attempt to
underline Gorbachev's new policy; Gorbachev himself was a candidate member
at the time.) This theme was taken up by Mr Shevardnadze in March 1989.
Outlining the future of Soviet foreign policy, he said that the new Congress
of People's Deputies could play an important role as matters could be debated
by the whole parliament. Shevarnadze pointed out that, had this been the way
of operating in 1979, Soviet troops would not have been sent into Afghanistan.
He even went so far as to suggest that referenda and public opinion polls could
be held before important foreign policy decisions were taken. This gave official
blessing to the idea of making Soviet foreign policy publicly accountable. This
was first seriously considered in 1988, most notably in an article in *Pravda* in
August, in which political commentator Vsevolod Ovchinnikov called for the
widest possible discussion of foreign policy matters. He declared: "The people
should play an active part in the formation of Soviet foreign policy. Pluralism
of opinions is not a luxury, it is not a tribute to fashion, but a way of arriving
at the best decisions, of avoiding mistakes or at least being able to put them
right in time."

So is Soviet foreign policy now dictated by a desire to show the world
that the Russian bear is in fact a cuddly creature and not the grizzly animal
it seemed under Brezhnev and Gromyko? To some extent, yes. But, as with
all of Gorbachev's policies, there is also a more pragmatic approach.

Firstly, he sees the need for Marxism-Leninism to adapt to the times. The
economies of the developed capitalist countries have not fallen into decline,
and in many ways are healthier than those of the socialist world. At the

Communist Party plenum on agriculture in March 1989 Gorbachev admitted that not only is the USSR not producing enough food to feed its population, but the gap between the Soviet Union and the capitalist countries in all areas of agricultural output is widening. While such a situation exists, it is nonsense to expect countries to adopt the Soviet system. Sorting out domestic problems, particularly agriculture, is Gorbachev's primary concern. The old adage that foreign policy is born out of domestic policy has never been truer than it is for the Soviet Union today.

Another legacy of the Brezhnev era is the vicious circle of ever-greater spending on arms to the detriment of the welfare of the Soviet citizen. In order to maintain its superpower status, the Soviet Union had to keep its armed forces strong. This left less available for spending on domestic needs. Whilst the need to maintain the security of the USSR remains a priority of Soviet foreign policy, the Soviet leadership has clearly recognized that this can still be achieved with smaller armed forces than currently exist. By reversing the trend of recent years and announcing a reduction in the size of the armed forces by 500,000 men, Gorbachev has not only won world-wide acclaim, he has also made a significant step towards channelling resources towards the civilian sector at home. Furthermore, by choosing the United Nations as his stage he confirmed Soviet policy to raise the UN's profile as a body for the resolution of international disputes. Whether it is seen, then, as New Political Thinking, or whether it is simply coming to terms with reality, Soviet foreign policy has entered a qualitatively different phase.

LOOKING WESTWARDS

No area of Soviet foreign policy has been more closely monitored than the USSR's relations with "the West", specifically the capitalist countries of Western Europe and the USA and Canada. This is the area where military superpower meets military superpower, and where if negotiations failed and war occurred the whole world would suffer. In the 1970s it seemed that detente had brought with it a new era of improved East-West relations. But as disagreements about arms control and human rights started to call into question the new-found warmth between the two sides, the Soviet intervention in Afghanistan in December 1979 plunged relations into a new cold war era. When Ronald Reagan became US President in 1981 his blatantly anti-communist attitude suggested that a new thaw would be a long time in coming.

It is fortunate for both East and West that Mikhail Gorbachev saw the need for an improvement in relations. But it would be wrong to portray him as the saviour of the East-West dialogue and the sole creator of a new detente. Many Western leaders have long been prepared for greater dialogue with the Soviet Union. Gorbachev has now demonstrated that there is a willingness to improve relations from the Soviet side, too. But the difficulty for Western leaders now is that, having spent so long waiting at the starting point for someone to run with, they have been caught cold and overtaken by Gorbachev in his efforts to show the world that he is serious about improving relations.

What makes it more difficult for Western leaders now to settle to definite negotiations with the USSR on all matters of disagreement, is that Gorbachev has taken Western public opinion with him. Compared to the years of Brezhnevite "stagnation" (the term applies equally well to Soviet foreign policy as it does to domestic affairs) in a short space of time Gorbachev has produced such a flood of proposals on arms control, human rights and mutual co-operation and security that the West barely knows which way to turn before encountering another proposal. This makes a reasoned response difficult.

But does this suggest that the Soviet leader's proposals are simply designed for propaganda value? Not at all. There can be little doubt that the New Political Thinking of the Soviet leadership encompasses a genuine desire for increased contacts with the West and greater mutual understanding. Clearly there is an important economic element involved. Improved relations with the West will, it is hoped, bring more foreign investment into the Soviet Union, thus improving the state of the domestic economy and helping the chances of *perestroika* at home. One of the main obstacles to this is not so much Western caution as the non-convertability of the rouble. If the Soviet Union wishes to establish widespread economic relations with Western companies it cannot rely on a barter system of trade, such as the "vodka-cola" deals of the 1970s.

Going into the 1990s, the key areas for improvement in relations between the Soviet Union and the West remain the questions of arms control, human rights and mutual co-operation and security. Soviet admissions of superiority in arms and that their military policy in the past could have been construed by the West as being threatening are signs of the new realism. The release of many prisoners of conscience and Moscow's desire to hold a human rights' conference in 1991, show that previous Western concerns for human rights in the USSR were well-founded, but that in this area, too, the Soviet Union is prepared to be more honest. The genuine cuts in military manpower and equipment announced by Gorbachev at the United Nations in December 1988, and the willingness to enter into new dialogue on arms reductions at Vienna in 1989 illustrates that in its relations with the West the Soviet Union wants to move away from confrontation to consolidation. And, although undoubtedly inspired in part by a Soviet desire that Eastern Europe is not isolated when the EC countries pull closer together in 1992, Gorbachev's talk of "a common European home", in which the USA and Canada also have a role, should not be dismissed out of hand. After years of an aggressive Soviet foreign policy Western leaders are right to be cautious of Gorbachev's proposals, and to keep a careful eye on how much he is able to achieve. But if this caution overflows into suspicion and hostility, then an opportunity for a qualitative improvement in East-West relations will have been lost.

WOOING THE ORIENT

"The Soviet Union is also an Asia-Pacific country. The vast region's complex problems are familiar to it; it is directly touched by them." So said Mikhail Gorbachev in a speech in Vladivostok in July 1986. The speech marked a turning point in Soviet attitudes to the Far East, and served as a reminder to the rest of the world that, whilst the most heavily-populated ares of the Soviet Union are in Europe, the majority of the country lies in Asia. Gorbachev signalled in Vladivostok that the Soviet Union is keen to develop its relations with all countries in Asia and the Pacific Basin. But by far the most important of these is China, the world's other huge socialist state and the country with whom the USSR has a 7,500 km land border.

China reacted coolly to the 1986 proposals for improved bilateral relations, remaining firm on what they considered to be "the three obstacles" to normalization. These were for the withdrawal of Soviet forces from Afghanistan, the withdrawal of Soviet-backed Vietnamese troops from Cambodia and a reduction in Soviet troops on the Sino-Soviet border. At the same time the Chinese leadership began to show signs that, given satisfactory progress on these issues, they would be prepared to confine to history the ideological disputes between Mao Tse Tung and Khrushchev which led to the souring of relations in the late 1950s and early 1960s.

Developments in 1988 paved the way for the normalization of relations. The pull-out from Afghanistan began. With soviet backing, Vietnam announced that it would withdraw its troops from Cambodia. Two Soviet divisions were removed from Mongolia and, in his speech at the United Nations, Gorbachev announced a reduction of 200,000 Soviet troops in the Far East. Under the terms of a further agreement with the Mongolian Government, the USSR agreed to withdraw three quarters of its forces stationed there. As a further indication of its desire to re-establish good relations with China, the Soviet Union announced that military formations deployed on the Sino-Soviet border would be re-formed "to a defensive structure". This last point reflects a general desire by the political leadership to show the world that the Soviet armed forces exist solely for defensive reasons. But whilst this may sound attractive politically, it does not make military sense, since any army is ineffective if it cannot carry out offensive operations in response to an enemy attack.

The improving cultural and scientific exchanges which continued through this period were accompanied by an increase in diplomatic activity. An agreement was reached in December 1986 to open a Chinese consulate in Leningrad and a Soviet one in Shanghai. Contacts between foreign ministers increased, culminating in the visit of Qian Qichen to Moscow in December 1988—the first such visit in 30 years—and Eduard Shevardnadze's trip to Beijing in February 1989. This was the first ever visit by a Soviet foreign minister to the People's Republic of China. As well as creating a better atmosphere for the future development of relations, the main achievement of these meetings was the decision to hold a Sino-Soviet summit in Beijing in May 1989—the first such since Khrushchev visited China in 1959. This will see the re-establishment of ties between the two communist parties, severed in 1966 when Mao refused to send a delegation to the 23rd Soviet Party Congress. The summit is not expected to be concluded by the signing of an alliance between the two countries, as it is recognized that such a move could worry the West and place an unnecessary strain on both countries' relations with the USA and Western Europe.

Aside from China, the most interesting aspect of the Soviet Union's developing relations with the Far East is the question of relations with Japan. Economically and technologically, the Soviet Union is keen to encourage Japanese involvement in its development. But fundamental problems remain. At the very heart of Soviet-Japanese relations is the issue of the Kurile Islands. Because of these four islands, which were seized by the Soviet Union in 1945, the two countries haves till not signed a peace treaty after the Second World War. Until this is done, no significant deals on co-operation can come into force; and Japan continues to insist that the only satisfactory solution will be the return of the islands to them. For the USSR, of course, the issue is not as simple as just handing back a few small pieces of land in the Pacific Ocean. To give away any land which is now considered as Soviet territory would be to risk similar claims on other parts of the country. China could claim parts of Siberia; in Europe, Romania could claim what is now the Soviet republic of

Moldavia. And, most significantly of all, areas such as the Baltic Republics of Estonia, Latvia and Lithuania could make still louder calls for a return to the pre-1940 situation of total independence. Once again, domestic considerations dictate the conduct of foreign policy.

Even if the question of the Kurile Islands were solved, there are still large obstacles to be faced before real developments could happen in Soviet-Japanese relations. The Soviet Union would like to see greater Japanese investment in the USSR, but Japan insists that for this to happen the Soviet Union must create a convertible rouble. Soviet economists recognize that this will take at least 10 years. The Japanese have responded coolly to Soviet overtures to sign agreements on the environment, increased tourism and the peaceful use of space. There is a feeling in Moscow that some members of the Japanese leadership believe that the greater willingness to co-operate which has become a hallmark of Soviet foreign policy will not permit the USSR to leave relations with Japan in abeyance, and that they will be forced at the very least into an agreement to cede the Kurile Islands. Such hopes seem premature. The Soviet Union may be keen to broaden its relations with the world, but it is not so desperate to do this at any price.

A ROLE IN THE MIDDLE EAST

Nowhere in the world is the new thinking in Soviet foreign policy better shown than in the Middle East. The Soviet Union has realized that sticking to purely ideological considerations cost them dearly in the region. Eduard Shevardnadze's five-nation trip to the Middle East in February 1989 showed that Moscow is keen to make up for the mistakes and lost opportunities of the past by bouncing right back to centre stage. To what extent they will succeed in doing this depends as much upon the USA and Israel as the Arab nations.

The crux of the new Soviet policy towards the Middle East is a recognition that the countries of the region no longer have to declare themselves as capitalist or socialist, nor openly ally themselves with the USA or the USSR. Moscow is no longer seeking to make the area one of superpower rivalry but one of co-operation to ensure a lasting peace. Crucial to this is the issue of Soviet-Israeli relations. The Soviet Union severed diplomatic ties with Israel as a result of the 1967 Arab-Israeli War, but is now making it clear that it believes the re-establishment of relations would be desirable for both sides.

Sporting and cultural links with Israel have been stepped up—in January

Israel's national basketball team played in Moscow, an event impossible just a couple of years ago. The USSR is showing more concern for its Jewish population. The opening in early 1989 of a Jewish cultural centre in Moscow, with the promise of a second one in Leningrad, comes at a time when Jewish emigration from the Soviet Union has been permitted to rise to the highest level for 60 years. Meetings between Shevardnadze and his Israeli counterpart Moshe Arens have become more frequent, the most notable being their encounter in Cairo in February. On the other side, the Soviet Union had a hand in persuading the Palestine Liberation Organization in November 1988 publicly to accept the existence of the State of Israel.

But this does not imply that the Soviet Union is prepared to sacrifice all to re-establish diplomatic links with Israel. As Japan is finding in the Far East, so Israel can see that the new realism in Soviet foreign policy is not simply a desire to be friends with everyone. In any case, bending over backwards to please Israel would not win the support of the Arab countries and the Soviet Union's main concern in the Middle East is to achieve a lasting settlement and maintain good relations with all parties. The sticking point at present is the question of an international peace conference on the Middle East. Until such a meeting is convened the re-establishment of diplomatic ties is out of the question.

Shevardnadze seized the initiative whilst visiting Jordan by proposing a three-point plan in preparation for the conference. It underlines also Moscow's desire to see a new and more significant role in world affairs given to the United Nations. The first point is to convene a meeting of the five permanent members of the UN Security Council—the USA, the USSR, China, France and Britain—at foreign minister level. After discussions with all parties concerned, these countries would then set up a preparatory body for the conference. The third stage would involve the UN Secretary-General, who would aim to bring all parties together within a time limit of six to nine months. By putting down concrete proposals the Soviet Union has shown that it has come back onto the Middle East stage as a serious player. The growing support of the USA and Britain for Israeli recognition of the PLO and of the need for the conference also helps to strengthen the Soviet position.

How can the Arab nations be expected to react to Moscow's initiatives in the area? After all, President Sadat's expulsion of Soviet military technicians and advisers from Egypt in July 1972 virtually signalled the end of Soviet involvement in the Middle East peace process, and the Soviet involvement in Afghanistan damaged their relations with the Moslem world. But Shevardnadze's visit to the Middle East, coming hard on the heels of the completion of the Soviet withdrawal from Afghanistan, seems to have opened up genuine possibilities for improved contacts with the Arab states which will be mutually beneficial. This was not Moscow begging forgiveness for past errors and trying to ease Washington out of the area; this was a new start and a recognition of the reality of the situation. Particularly indicative of this was Shevardnadze's visit to Cairo. Furthermore, his meeting there with Mr Arens was a recognition of the role Egypt has already played in the peace process, and an endorsement of her policy of being the only Arab country to have recognized Israel.

The Soviet desire to play a part in achieving lasting peace between Iran and Iraq was evident in the Foreign Minister's visits to these two countries, and his audience with the Ayatollah Khomeini showed that, after the Soviet withdrawal from Afghanistan, Iran is prepared to conduct a serious dialogue with the Soviet Union. Moscow will not even have been upset by the Ayatollah's suggestion that she adopt Islam as the answer to her problems!

There are even signs that Syria, the Soviet Union's traditional ally in the area, can be persuaded by Moscow to soften its stance towards Israel and its Arab neighbours in the interests of a lasting settlement to both the Arab-Israeli question and the Gulf situation. The USSR is continuing to lean on President Assad to accept the more conciliatory line towards Israel being shown by Yasser Arafat, (Syria has supported the more radical Palestinian factions) as well as trying to encourage Damascus to patch up its relations with Egypt and Iraq. Syria is keen to play a part in the Middle East peace process and may well find that the only way in which she can do this is to follow the line that Moscow is now preaching. Syria is also finding that Soviet military support is not as forthcoming as it once was. The USSR is continuing to demand Syrian repayment of its $15 billion military debt, and it seems that the visit of Soviet Defence Minister Yazov to Damascus in March 1989 was more a way of underlining the new reality than any promise of an increase in military support.

What the new Soviet policy towards the Middle East is showing is that Moscow has learned from past mistakes and is not afraid to take a new initiative in a spirit of compromise and co-operation to ensure herself a place in the region's future.

GREATER FREEDOM FOR SOCIALISM?

An ironic anecdote used to be told in Prague that Czechoslovakia was the most neutral country in the world, because its government did not even interfere in the country's own domestic policy! Certainly events such as the Soviet invasion of Hungary in 1956 and the crushing by Soviet tanks of the Prague Spring in 1968 gave the countries of Eastern Europe in particular the idea that they had no alternative but to follow Moscow's dictates in all ares of policy. But as the twenty-first century comes closer, Moscow has recognized that the world is a very different place from that of the '50s or '60s. The developing countries have not turned automatically to socialism as Marxism-Leninism once held that they would do. And the retreat of the Soviet Army from Afghanistan with its tail between its legs has taught both the leadership in Moscow and the Soviet people that not only does a policy of sending in the tanks not guarantee the success of the revolution, it also convinces the rest of the world that the Soviet Union is an aggressor which must be opposed at every turn.

The Soviet Union's socialist allies are reacting to the new political thinking in Soviet foreign policy in different ways, and it seems that if Moscow really is to win and hold the trust of the rest of the world then she dare not interfere to ensure that her allies adapt themselves to *perestroika*. The Czechoslovak leadership finds itself in a particular quandary. Brought to power by the Soviet backlash which removed the reformers in 1968, they would deny their own legitimacy if they were to admit that the Soviet actions then were a mistake. A few efforts have been made to tinker with the system, but these are far from Gorbachev's *perestroika* ideal. But the idea of Moscow intervening by force to introduce into Czechoslovakia the kind of reforms which she stopped in 1968 is too ludicrous to bear serious consideration. East Germany finds itself in a similar situation. When the ideas of *perestroika* first started to take shape in the Soviet Union, East German leader Erich Honecker declared that, just because your neighbour changes his wallpaper, it does not mean that you have to. The policies of the German Democratic Republic, then, remain largely untouched by *perestroika*; but, given the country's geographical location on the Warsaw Pact's central front with NATO, this will not dismay Moscow too greatly for the time being.

The only East European country which looks poised to take advantage of the new mood of Soviet foreign policy is Hungary. Having introduced mass multi-candidate elections in 1985, four years before the Soviet Union, Hungary has now announced that by the end of 1990 a multi-party system will be operating. Even though Gorbachev continued to stress after the Soviet Union's multi-candidate elections to the Congress of People's Deputies in March 1989 that there was no need for such a system in the USSR, the Soviet Union will not intervene either by force or even by pressure to prevent the Hungarians from choosing this path forward. And it was a relaxed Karoly Grosz who announced to the Central Committee of the Hungarian Party after his visit to Moscow in the same month that Gorbachev had declared that all possible safeguards should be provided so that no external force could interfere in the domestic affairs of socialist countries. The so-called "Brezhnev Doctrine", under the terms of which the Soviet Union virtually had *carte blanche* to intervene if it felt that one of its socialist allies was straying from the true path, is apparently dead.

Further afield, Moscow seems to be adopting a policy more akin to moral support for the countries of socialism. Whilst it is unlikely that the Soviet Union would abandon all its aid commitments to its friends among the developing countries, they are likely to find the almost bottomless pit of Soviet financial aid now has its limits. And with the Soviet armed forces being hit by cuts which will see tank factories turning out tractors, the Soviet Union is unlikely to risk the accusation that it is involved in upping the arms race in the Third World by supplying more weapons than before.

Vietnam has already been leant on to withdraw its troops from Cambodia, and Cuba has pulled her troops out of Angola, leaving the Soviet-backed government there to begin negotiations to end the civil war in the way it sees best. Military aid to Mozambique has been cut and there is talk, encouraged by the Americans, of ending Soviet support for the Sandinistas in Nicaragua. Overall the policy seems to be, as *Pravda's* political commentator Vsevolod Ovchinnikov put it, to allow the fulfilment of "the desire of the liberated countries of Asia, Africa and Latin America to play an independent role in history". In some cases this may seem like a cynical washing of Soviet hands at a time when problems for the country concerned had become massive. That could certainly be an interpretation of the Soviet withdrawal from Afghanistan. But the new realism does not deny that in some countries the path ahead will be tough and often bloody. And some of these countries may still opt for a socialist way ahead. The difference now is that, if they do so, Moscow will be standing on the sidelines and applauding but will not wade in to dirty her own boots—or the newly found idea that Soviet foreign policy may genuinely be peace-loving.

Independence Day Demonstration in Tallinn, Estonia (*Y. Goligorsky*)

In a Siberian doorway (*Angus Macqueen*)

REPORTAGE

THE ART OF SHOPPING

Angus Macqueen

The cow's carcass lies in the brown snow behind Novosibirsk food store no. 21. In Siberian winters there is little need for cold storage. A woman, in what must once have been a white coat, stands wielding a large cleaver and hacks away another section of ribs on a thick stump of birch wood. Chunks of pale meat pile up outside the shop's back door. Inside customers—I am the only man—wait patiently. Some peer optimistically at the stacks of cans, bottles and brown unlabelled boxes; some talk in undertones; most stand, string bag in hand, lost deep in their scarves, heavy coats and fur hats. Only a break in the intricate laws of the queue, or the attempted intrusion of war veterans and heroes of labour, who occasionally sell their right to jump queues as a professional service, causes a rumpus. Claims to have single-handedly saved Moscow from the Germans get little truck from women, who look as if they did.

This is my monthly meat ritual. Small blue and orange ration cards are presented, stamped and signed away at one desk; roubles handed over at another, before a final queue produces the prize: a brown paper bag. This contains the month's kilo of fresh—if frozen—meat and ½ kilo of butter. People rarely look inside the bag, or try to complain about the piece they have received: they know they would be risking serious abuse from the saleswomen, a dangerous species, and as often as not from the other customers, who cannot believe such naivety. Basically the queue fears it will just have to wait longer, with little chance of the complaint being met.

Shops, dependent on central supply and never in control of either quantity or quality, are grey and unappetizing, dank and underlit. Half the neon tubes are missing, don't work or flicker uncertainly over a slush brown concrete floor and a collection of crates and wire cages. There is no role for seductive packaging or the hard sell. The only musak squeals from a check-out woman's transistor perched on the unused till, next to the ubiquitous, and always employed, abacus. The wire cages—full of neatly stacked goods—are of little interest: usually they contain tins of fish in varieties of oil and tomato sauce, brown bags of rice and macaroni or dry biscuits. Desirable products—sausage, cheese or fruit, however, expensive, sell out almost before they are delivered, certainly before they reach a shelf.

Shopping is an art in Soviet life. It should be: women on average spend three hours a day practising it—before, during and after work. The cardinal rules become second nature. First get into the queue before bothering to find out what it is for; if people are queuing then there must be something more than macaroni at the far end. Next: never stand in just one queue; the really expert can manage three or more at a time, and not all in the same shop. The skill is in judging how fast any particular queue will move; the unskilled—those who return just too late—get scant sympathy from those coming on behind. Who knows how much there is left?

For reasons no doubt apparent it is worth getting to know shop assistants or warehouse men. They can give warning of impending deliveries the night before, or themselves will often syphon off the prize goods beforehand. Better still—find a railway worker. Whole trains have been known to disappear into the blizzards.

Such contacts are vital for this remains a barter economy. Influence, access and status, not income, are what really count—the world of Gogol's *Government Inspector* lives on. I have felt myself develop that gentle bow and dab of the forelock, nothing too obsequious, in front of those who decide or provide. A fine salami for the nurse to ensure clean sheets on the hospital bed; caviar to the booking clerk to ensure the holiday in the Crimea; caviar onwards to ensure the booking clerk's child get into the better class at school. The teacher . . . well she, in a quite inexcusable, but fortunately habitual, fit of extravagance washes the caviar down with a precious bottle of vodka. I help. Nearly everyone has some service or access they can offer; nearly everyone has a price. Bribery and corruption? "Never," you will be told, "Just the way the system works".

Attempts to clear "corruption"—and Gorbachev's is not the first—go to the heart of the way normal people—not just corrupt officialdom—have found to survive, without providing an alternative. On the one hand this makes the leader popular in that few like the overt corpulent excess of the "mafia" years. On the other, squeaky clean means creaky—indeed non-operational; there is no oil to help the mismatched parts find a way of working together.

"What the hell am I supposed to do now?" swore a friend of mine, when he discovered his regular—blackmarket—supply of spare parts for the car had dried up. His friend had been caught selling them on the side; he had been fined and fired. "Look for another friend," I replied rather too smugly. No spare parts meant he could not drive me home through the −25 °C cold. My toes were soon firm believers in backhanders, and I understood only too well popular disquiet at the prospect of further dislocation brought about by economic reform. The centre's claim that "There is no other way"—to coin a phrase—wears only so thin.

SONGS OF GOD AND REVOLUTION

Helen Womack

The entrance is unpromising. Bored teenagers smoke, leaning against a notice board with yellowing Communist Party posters and a smell of lavatories drifts across the ground floor of the factory club. But go up the stairs past the caretaker's office and suddenly, from behind a door down the corridor, you will hear the liquid sound of Svetlana Dagayeva's soprano voice. She is warming up for a rehearsal of Rospev, an amateur Moscow choir which specializes in singing Russian church and early music.

The director is Andrei Lazarev, a professional singer and choir master, who gives his time twice a week to this motley group of schoolteachers, doctors and office workers for love of the music and desire to share it. "O, O, O, not aaah, you do not know the Russian language, you sound like a provincial fishwife!" he shouts at Anya, a middle-aged paediatrician, who has been coming to rehearsals for two years and is still as hopeless as ever. But he would never dream of throwing her out and she takes his abuse in good part because he is such a fine musician.

The piece Anya was butchering was "Who Can Separate Me From The Love Of God?", an anonymous seventeenth century cantata of spellbinding beauty. Rospev sings a range of music from chants by Ivan the Terrible to choral works by eighteenth century composers. Who in the West has heard of Bortnyansky, Diletsky or Degtyaryov? Yet arguably their work is as fine as that of Haydn. Now, partly as a result of the widening tolerance for religion under *perestroika*, such music is enjoying a revival in Russia, as the enthusiastic audiences at Rospev's concerts testify.

The singers may practise in drab surroundings, with a portrait of Lenin glaring down on them in their rehearsal room. They may arrive late for these sessions, loaded down with shopping bags or burdened with work problems. Veronika is tired of the young monsters in her secondary school class, Svetlana must give up her summer holidays to supervize children in a pioneer camp . . . But when they step out on stage—mostly in churches converted into museums—they are transformed. The men, dressed year-in, year-out in the same scruffy sweaters and jeans, manage to get from somewhere black jackets and dickie bows. The women wear full-length black dresses sparkling with sequins which they have sewn themselves.

They perform among the icons and gold of the Russian Orthodox Church. Lenin, Stalin and Khrushchev did their best to wipe it out, Gorbachev is allowing it a limited renaissance. But throughout the years of Communism, many Russians have remained faithful to the church, theology apart, because it has been an island of beauty in the wilderness of concrete and materialism.

The church is at the centre of growing Russian national consciousness. Because the Russians have been the dominant ethnic group in the Soviet Union, other embittered nationalities such as the Baltic peoples tend to forget that Russian culture has also suffered under Soviet power. One member of the choir tells how his grandmother, who spent 17 years in labour camp and internal exile for giving a night's shelter to a priest, was reduced by lack of access to a church to baptising her grandson in a washing-up bowl in the kitchen. Rospev, like a number of unofficial heritage groups which have sprung up in the last few years, expresses a legitimate longing for roots and lost values. It is very far from the unacceptable face of Russian nationalism—the pan-Slav and overtly anti-semitic Pamyat movement.

"Soviet people are just so uncultured," complains Veronika with a typical schoolteacher's despair at the prevailing ignorance and lack of taste. She has not been to the West and naively assumes our standards are higher. But one sees what she means when Rospev enters a choral competition. Entrants must show their repertoire of "revolutionary" music so the choir wittily opts for a programme of songs from the French Revolution.

The audience is appreciative, welcoming the contrast between Rospev and the act which preceded it, a chorus of plump women from a textile factory swathed in red crimplene and raucuous in their rendering of the Internationale. But the spectators reserve their loudest applause for an all-male ensemble from a physics institute who crown their performance of folk songs with a mime of rope pulling in time to the Volga Boat Song. Grandiose and vulgar, the presentation is essentially Soviet. Inevitably the judges award it first prize. Rospev comes a respectable fourth.

REFERENCE SECTION

POPULATION

Total population at the start of 1988 was officially estimated at 284,500,000 at a density of 12.7 per sq km. Annual growth rate during 1980–87 amounted to 1 per cent. As of 1986 the four largest population centres were:

Moscow	8,703,00
Leningrad	4,901,000
Kiev	2,495,000
Tashkent	2,073,000

POLITICAL STRUCTURE

Under the 1977 Constitution, the Union of Soviet Socialist Republics (USSR) is formally a federal state comprising 15 Union (constituent) Republics of equal status, voluntarily linked and having the right to secede. By far the largest of these is the Russian Federation. There are also Autonomous Republics (16 within the Russian Federation and four in three other Union Republics), Autonomous Regions (five within the Russian Federation and one each in three other Union Republics), and National Districts (10, all in the Russian Federation). The following make up the 15 Union Republics:

Name	Area (sq km)
Armenia	29,800
Azerbaijan	86,600
Byelorussia	207,600
Estonia	45,100
Georgia	69,700
Kazakhstan	2,717,300
Kirghiz	198,500
Latvia	63,700
Lithuania	65,200
Moldavia	33,700
Russia	17,075,400
Tadzhikistan	143,100

Turkmenistan	488,100
Ukraine	603,700
Uzbekistan	447,400

Wide-ranging constitutional reforms announced at the end of 1988 heralded a drastic restructuring of the state political system, placing far greater power and influence in the hands of democratically elected authorities.

PRE-1989 SYSTEM

While effective authority remained in the hands of the Communist Party, the highest organ of state power was the USSR Supreme Soviet (*Verkhovnyi Soviet SSSR*), which consisted of two chambers with 750 deputies in each. Both houses had equal rights and powers, were elected simultaneously but separately, and their terms ran concurrently. Deputies were directly elected by secret ballot from single lists of candidates for five-year terms by universal adult suffrage. The right to nominate candidates was exercised by the Communist Party of the Soviet Union (CPSU), trade unions, the All-Union Leninist Young Communist League (*Komsomol*), co-operatives and other organizations, labour collectives and meetings of military servicemen.

The Soviet of the Union (Soviet Soyuza) was elected from single-member constituencies of approximately equal size (300,000 inhabitants) under an absolute majority system, with further ballots being held where no absolute majority is obtained. The Soviet of Nationalities (Soviet Natsionalnostyei) was elected from constituencies organized so that the chamber comprises 32 deputies from each Union Republic, 11 from each Autonomous Republic, five from each Autonomous Region and one from each National District. At a joint session the members elected the Presidium of the Supreme Soviet to serve as the legislature's permanent organ. The Presidium, led by a chairman, functions as a collective head of state. The Supreme Soviet also appointed the Council of Ministers, headed by a Chairman, to form the executive and administrative branch of government.

Each of the Union Republics has a constitution and state structure modelled on that of the central administration, with a unicameral Supreme Soviet, a Presidium and a Council of Ministers to deal with internal affairs. The Chairmen of the Presidiums are ex officio Vice-Chairmen of the Presidium of the USSR Supreme Soviet, while the Chairmen of the Councils of Ministers of the Union Republics are ex officio members of the USSR Council of Ministers. The deputies to the Supreme Soviets of the Union Republics are all elected in single-member constituencies, not normally at the same time as the USSR Supreme Soviet elections.

CONSTITUTIONAL AMENDMENTS AND THE NEW SYSTEM OF GOVERNMENT

The Supreme Soviet approved a law on electoral reform, together with a series of amendments to the 1977 Constitution, on Nov. 29–Dec. 1, 1988. The main points of the amendments are summarized below.

The USSR Congress of People's Deputies and the USSR Supreme Soviet. "The higher body of state authority of the USSR" would be a newly created Congress of People's Deputies. The "exclusive prerogatives" of this body would include: (i) the adoption and amendment of the USSR Constitution; (ii) "the adoption of resolutions on matters of the national-state structure within the jurisdiction of the USSR"; (iii) the definition of the state border and ratification of changes in borders between republics; (iv) the definition of "basic guidelines" of Soviet domestic and foreign policy; the ratification of long-term state economic plans; (vi) the election of the USSR Supreme Soviet; (vii) the election of the Chairman and the First Deputy Chairman of the USSR Supreme Soviet (head and deputy head of state); and (viii) the ratification of the Chairman of the USSR Council of Ministers (Prime Minister).

The Congress of People's Deputies would consist of 2,250 deputies: 750 from territorial constituencies with a roughly equal number of voters; 750 from "national-territorial" constituencies organized to give representation to the Soviet Union's ethnic groups—32 from each union republic (SSR), 11 from each autonomous republic (ASSR), five from each autonomous *oblast* (region) and one from each national *okrug* (district); and 750 from all-union social organizations. Regular sessions of the Congress of People's Deputies would be held once a year.

The Supreme Soviet would consist, as hitherto, of two numerically equal chambers—the Soviet of the Union and the Soviet of Nationalities—which would include deputies from social organizations. The Supreme Soviet would convene for much longer regular spring and autumn sessions, each lasting for three to four months "as a rule". While the constitutional amendments transferred some of the Supreme Soviet's functions to the new Congress, they also made explicit the role of the Supreme Soviet in many areas where responsibility had hitherto been exercised by the Presidium.

The Supreme Soviet's power would include (i) the appointment of the Chairman of the Council of Ministers and the ratification of the composition of the Council; (ii) the formation of the Defence Council, ratification of its composition, and appointments to the Supreme Command of the armed forces; (iii) ensuring "the uniformity of legislative regulations" throughout the USSR and laying "the foundations for legislation" at the state level and in union republics; (iv) implementing legislative regulation of property relations and the "procedure for the realization of the constitutional rights, freedoms and duties of citizens"; (v) ratifying or abrogating international treaties; (vi) determining "basic measures" in the defence sphere and proclaiming mobilization or a state of war; (vii) making decisions on the use of the armed forces "in the event of the need to meet international treaty obligations"; (viii) repealing decrees or resolutions of the Presidium of the Supreme Soviet or orders of the Chairman of the Supreme Soviet; and (ix) repealing resolutions or orders made by union republic councils of ministers "in the event of their not being in keeping with the Constitution".

The Presidium of the Supreme Soviet would, among other things: (i) "ensure that the constitutions and laws of the union republics conform with the constitution and laws"; and (ii) declare where necessary a state of martial law or emergency "for the whole country and also in particular localities—with mandatory examination of this matter with the Presidium of the Supreme Soviet of the relevant union republic". (In such cases "special forms of administration" by USSR and republic state bodies might be introduced.)

The Chairman of the USSR Supreme Soviet—the state President. A new executive state presidency would be established under the title of Chairman of the USSR Supreme Soviet, elected by the Congress of People's Deputies by secret ballot for a five-year term and for not more than two successive terms. The Chairman might be recalled at any time by secret ballot of the congress. The Chairman's duties would include: (i) exercising "overall leadership" in the preparation of matters for examination by the USSR Congress of People's Deputies and Supreme Soviet; (ii) submitting to the Congress candidates for election to the post of First Deputy Chairman of the Supreme Soviet, and for appointment or election to the post of Chairman of the Council of Ministers and other leading posts; and (iii) heading the Defence Council.

A people's deputy to both the parliamentary bodies would have the right to put questions to the Chairman of the Supreme Soviet as well as to the Chairman of the Council of Ministers and other leading officials. Questions would have to be answered within three days.

A Committee for Supervision of the Constitution would be elected by the

Congress of People's Deputies, to include representatives from every union republic.

Recourse to Referendum. The "most important matters" of union-wide republican or local significance could be resolved by referendum on the decision of the relevant elected body.

The Electoral System. One third of the deputies to USSR and republic parliamentary bodies would be elected from "social organizations" such as the CPSU, trade unions, the Leninist Young Communist League (*Komsomol*), co-operative organizations and creative unions. These deputies would be elected directly by the delegates to the congresses of these organizations or by the participants in plenums of their all-union or republican leadership bodies. Ballot papers might include any number of candidates.

The constitutional pattern established by the amendments would be replicated in full in all the union republics (but with their Supreme Soviets remaining unicameral).

THE COMMUNIST PARTY

Communist Party of the Soviet Union (CPSU, Kommunisticheskaya Partiya Sovietskogo Soyuza). The CPSU traces its descent from the Russian Social Democratic Labour Party (founded in 1898, which in 1903 split into supporters and opponents of the concept of the party as a highly centralized vanguard of professional revolutionaries, the former becoming known as Bolsheviks ("majoritarians") and the latter as Mensheviks ("minoritarians"). The Bolshevik wing established itself as a separate party in 1912, was legalized in Russia following the overthrow of the monarchy in March 1917, and seized power from the provisional government in a *coup d'état* in November of that year. Thereafter, the party changed its name to the Russian Communist Party (Bolshevik) in 1918, to the All-Union Communist Party (Bolshevik) in 1925, and to its present name in 1952.

OPPOSITION GROUPS

In recent years a number of other officially tolerated political organizations have emerged, most prominently in the Baltic Republics, where the Popular Fronts of Latvia and Estonia, and the Sajudis movement in Lithuania, all of which appear to command substantial support. Similar, albeit less powerful, organizations have sprung up in a number of other republics. The "Democratic Union", established in May 1988, has called for "economic and spiritual pluralism, a multi-party system, a legal opposition press and free trade unions".

Communist Party leaderships

General secretary: Mr Mikhail Gorbachev.

Full politburo members: Mr Mikhail Gorbachev, Mr Yegor Ligachev, Gen. Viktor Chebrikov, Mr Vadim Medvedev, Mr Viktor Nikonov, Mr Nikolai Ryzhkov, Mr Vladimar Shcherbitsky, Mr Eduard Shevardnadze, Mr Nikolai Slyunkov, Mr Vitaly Vorotnikov, Mr Aleksandr Yakovlev, Mr Lev Zaikov. Candidate members. Mrs Aleksandra Biryukova, Mr Anatoly Lukyanov, Yuri Maslyukov, Mr Georgy Razumovsky, Mr Yury Solovev, Mr Nikolai Talyzin, Mr Aleksandr Vlasov, Gen. Dmitry Yazov.

Central committee secretariat: Mr Mikhail Gorbachev, Gen. Viktor Chebrikov, Mr Lev Zaikov, Mr Yegor Ligachev, Mr Vadim Medvedev, Mr Viktor Nikonov, Mr Georgy Razumovsky, Mr Aleksandr Yakovlev, Mr Nikolai Slyunkov, Mr Oleg Bakhlanov.

Republican party leaders: Armenian CP—Mr Suren Arutyunyan; Azerbaijan CP—Mr Abdul Rakhman Vezirov; Byelorussian CP—Mr Yefrem Sokolov; Estonian CP—Mr Vaino Vaelaes, Georgian CP—Mr Givi Gumbaridze; Kazakh CP—Mr Gennady Kolbin; Kirghiz CP—Mr Absamat Masaliyev; Latvian CP—Mr Janis Vagris; Lithuanian CP—Mr Algirdas Brazauskas; Moldavian CP—Mr Semyon Grossu; Tadjik CP—Mr Kakhar Makhkamov; Turkmen CP— Mr Saparmurad Niyazov; Ukrainian CP—Mr Vladimir Shcherbitsky; Uzbek CP—Mr Rafik Nishanov.

INDEX